JOHN MEYENDORFF

THE VISION
OF
UNITY

ST VLADIMIR'S SEMINARY PRESS
CRESTWOOD, NEW YORK 10707
1987

Library of Congress Cataloging in Publication Data
Meyendorff, John, 1926-
  Vision of unity.

  1. Christian union—Orthodox Eastern Church.
2. Orthodox Eastern Church—Doctrines. 3. Orthodox Eastern
Church—Government. 4. Orthodox Eastern Church—United
States—History—20th century. 5. United States—Church history—
20th century. I. Title.
BX324.M48 1987   281.9   87-23495
ISBN 0-88141-068-3

THE VISION OF UNITY

© Copyright 1987

by

ST VLADIMIR'S SEMINARY PRESS

ISBN 0-88141-068-3

PRINTED IN THE UNITED STATES OF AMERICA
BY
ATHENS PRINTING COMPANY
New York, NY 10018-6401

THE VISION OF UNITY

Contents

II.
DEBATES ON CHURCH ORDER

Introduction

"I believe in One, Holy, Catholic and Apostolic Church." This fundamental confession, expressed in the Creed, has direct implications for the life of dioceses and parishes, for Orthodox witness before those who do not belong to the Church, for practical judgment about involvement in social and political issues, for attitudes one adopts towards one's own cultural background and towards the life of the world as a whole.

The author of the essays, gathered in this book, is a professional theologian, who has dedicated most of his life to teaching and to investigating the past of Christianity, studying the ways in which the faith of the Church was confessed throughout the ages by the Fathers of the Church. During a more recent period of exactly twenty years—from January 1965 to December 1984—the same author was also the Editor of a Church monthly, *The Orthodox Church*, in which he published signed editorials, reflecting upon the growth and development of Orthodoxy in America. For him, it was a blessed challenge. Indeed, he was forced to relate the permanent and unchanging faith of the Church to the changing circumstances of our recent history, and to the birth of a new Orthodox Church on the American continent.

One of the major lessons of the past is that, at all times—even at the time of the apostles, chosen by Christ Himself—the Christian faith was maintained and proclaimed by imperfect human beings. This is also the case for us. But this does not mean that the divine-human existence of the Holy Church—the pure Bride of Christ, His Body—in its holiness and its integrity, depends upon the sins and imperfections of its members. If that was the case, the Church, as a human in-

9

stitution, would long have ceased to be! Actually, the accumulation of human shortcomings in its visible history, is the best proof of its Divine origin and foundation: without Christ Himself being its head, we humans alone would have not been able to protect it from the fate of all perishable institutions.

In the Orthodox understanding the promise of Christ— "The gates of hell will not overcome it" (Mat 16:19)—applies to the Church as sacramental, eucharistic body, not to individual, local churches. It is a well-known historical fact, for example, that for centuries a prosperous church existed in North Africa (today's Tunisia and Algeria), where it was glorified by great Fathers (St Cyprian, St Augustine), by innumerable martyrs of the faith and by great feats of theology and art. But eventually that church disappeared completely. Similar total uprootings of Christian presence occurred more recently, for instance in Asia Minor, today's Turkey.

Perhaps, in these specific cases, the collapse of Christianity was not really a punishment for human shortcomings, but a result of historical catastrophes. Nevertheless, the total disappearance of a Christian presence in those particular areas reminds us that Christian mission is never endowed with an absolute guarantee of human success and permanence. This fact indeed applies to our own mission in America and it is our duty to avoid a disintegration of Orthodox Christianity within the secularistic melting pot of American society.

The editorials reprinted in this book ask the question: Can we survive in chaos and disunity? They are in two sections:

(1) The issue of Orthodox unity in America
(2) The basic principles of Church structure: The Church is a "conciliar" Church, the Church of all people, clergy and laity, old and young, men and women—the "catholic" Church, of all nations and generations.

Each of the editorials relates to events happening at the time of publication. For instance, a most significant event during the 1965-1985 period was the establishment of the autocephaly of the Orthodox Church in America on April

10, 1970. Opposition to this historical act, which was sealed by the signature of Patriarch Alexis of Moscow seven days before his death, came from those who did not believe that Orthodoxy had "come of age" in America, and also from those who did not possess that Orthodox vision of the Church, sanctioned by ecclesiology and canons, that requires that Orthodox Christians live and act as one Body, wherever they are. An age-long routine, which identifies the Church with ethnic cultures, and the vested interest of patriarchates abroad have delayed and still delay the movement towards Orthodox unity in America. It remains, however, that no real alternative to Autocephaly has been proposed by anyone who sincerely seeks Orthodox unity. Indeed, it is difficult to deny that Autocephaly, which is now available for those who want it, provides principles and structures, able to preserve the ethnic traditions wherever these are needed, and also to secure the gradual process leading to canonical unity and administrative coherence of the Orthodox Church in America.

The need for unity is further illustrated in the discussion of other issues of Church life, which appears in the essays. In spite of many shortcomings, the progress achieved in the past decades is impressive. Many of the problems which had plagued the Church in the twenties and thirties—particularly the artificial opposition between clergy and laity in managing ecclesiastical affairs—have been largely resolved (although they still persist in some ethnic jurisdictions): there is a real sense of conciliarity and co-responsibility, and those who complain about such issues can be referred to the All-American Councils, where clergy and laity share the same possibility to speak and to vote. The development of education, of printed resources, of books and periodicals allows for the Orthodox voice to be heard on the ecumenical scene with more coordination, less duplication and a greater sense of common purpose. With Orthodox unity realized all these achievements would be even more effective and fruitful, and a united American church would be of much more help to those who in Russia, in the Middle East, or in other areas of our troubled world, are deprived of those essential freedoms which make Americans justifiably proud of their country.

The editorials appear in this book essentially in their original form with only minor editorial corrections, and thus represent something of a personal journal. This explains some inevitable repetitions, and also the journalistic passion with which some pages are written.

The author wants to express particular gratitude to Stephen T. Kopestonsky, the managing editor of *The Orthodox Church,* who—during those twenty years of common work—patiently typed and edited all the texts included in this volume.

I.

STEPS TOWARDS UNITY

Unity of Orthodo..

Back in 1906 Archbishop Tikhon of America, who i. became Patriarch of Moscow, presented to the ecclesiastica. authorities in Russia the project of a united (autonomous or autocephalous) Church of America. Under the leadership of one archbishop, the various nationalities would have kept their own organizations and would have retained, of course, their customs and traditions. Since that time our Church has always based its ecclesiastical life on the assumption that this was the only possible canonical and practical future for Orthodoxy in America. And the All-American Sobor (1963) confirmed this desire to see Orthodoxy united and autocephalous in America.

There were a number of reasons why Archbishop Tikhon's project was not implemented: the Russian Church went through the tragedy of persecutions, followed by internal divisions; the Church in America lacked a leadership which would not be challenged; the "Mother Churches" of the various national groups wanted to "keep control" over their American branches, and in America itself nationalism and prejudice between the various groups prevailed over their desire to be together. All this was due to the fact that nobody was concerned with the *Church itself*, and everybody preferred to obey the interests of a group or of a national culture (often wrongly understood). Many simply followed the instinct of inertia.

It seems, however, that we are approaching a new period in the history of our Church. Practically everyone understands that the present situation cannot last. The Standing Conference of Orthodox Bishops is watched by millions of laymen with great expectation. Nothing, however, will be done unless all realize exactly *why* Orthodox Unity is necessary.

The reasons are spiritual, canonical and practical.

Spiritually, it is obvious that when we confess our belief in "One, Holy, Catholic and Apostolic Church," this belief is meant to be the guiding principle of our lives: God is one, the Lord Jesus Christ is one, and the Church must be one also. "National" churches can exist only inasmuch as they accept to submit their particular interests to that of the whole Body of Christ.

Canonically, the rules and canons of *all* churches strictly forbid the existence of parallel ecclesiastical organizations on the same territory.

Practically, the Orthodox witness in this country will be immensely strengthened if the three million Orthodox pray and work together; if others are able really to see in us the One True Church, and not a conglomeration of mutually exclusive factions; if we can all join our forces in the education of our youth.

February, 1965

"Mothers" and "Daughters"

The present situation of the Orthodox Church in the world may prove to be the most dramatic turning point in its entire history. In the Communist countries, and especially in the Soviet Union, the Church is being challenged by an atheistic system whose open aim is the total extinction of religious faith. In the Western world, Orthodoxy suffers disunity and canonical chaos. However, it is also obvious that the world *needs* Orthodoxy, as the true Christian faith, and that thousands and millions of men and women are ready to discover this Truth, if it were shown to them.

The conclusion is that the historical future of the Orthodox Church depends upon two factors: its survival in Eastern Europe, particularly in Russia, and its progress in the Western world, particularly in America.

We are unable to contribute much to the situation in Eastern Europe; however, the fate of the Church in the Western world is in our hands or rather *should be* in our hands. The canonical conditions of normal Church life are clearly spelled out by the tradition of the Church: everywhere, Orthodox Christians must constitute *one* Church, led by its own bishop and priests. Through its bishop, each Church must be in communion with the Church universal. All the institutions of the Church—patriarchates, metropolitan districts, autocephalics, archdioceses—exist in order to secure this essential order of the Church.

The tragedy of our times—and the origin of the canonical disorder in which we live—is that these institutions are being used for non-ecclesiastical purposes: patriarchates, while considered by some as infallible criteria of canonicity, are being used by the governments of the countries in which they are situated *as political tools*; archbishops and metropolitans consider themselves as national, and not ecclesiastical leaders. Meanwhile, Orthodox canon law does have provisions against those abuses: *it clearly requires that all ecclesiastical questions are to be solved in the area where they arise.* African bishops in the fifth century even excommunicated those who appealed "beyond the seas" to solve their problems. They would also certainly consider as highly uncanonical the fact that the Antiochian American Diocese, for example, should have its fate resolved by a Synod meeting in a foreign country thousands of miles away.

Our conclusion today is that our internal disunity and disorder in America will last until the time when the patriarchates—the "Mother Churches"—as well as their representatives here and all the other ecclesiastical institutions, will at last realize their proper function and will prove themselves able to perform it. For the time being, by simply demanding that we submit to them, they continue to divide the Church and, in fact, want only that we serve their interests—which *are not* the interests of the Church in America. *Their proper and obvious ecclesiastical duty is to urge and help American Orthodox to realize their unity* while at the same time preserving all the national traditions, languages and customs which need to be kept.

August-September, 1966

Towards One Orthodox Church In America

The progression of American Orthodoxy towards organizational unity is much too slow. While the vast majority of clergy and laity are ready for it, the movement is hampered by apathy, and also by the conscious ill-will of an influential minority.

Let us not deceive ourselves: the unity of Orthodoxy in this country is indeed the will of God. The elementary principles of our faith, the unanimity of our canonical tradition and simple common sense require it. Every action taken either by the "Mother Churches," or by the Standing Conference of Bishops, or by any representative of the clergy and laity, with the express goal of realizing unity will be "right" and "canonical," and all discussions about "canonicity" without unity are, for the most part, pharisaic and hypocritical.

Among the sister-Churches, the Moscow Patriarchate seems to be the only one to have proclaimed openly, two years ago, that its intention was to promote in America a Church which would be "one and autocephalous." This public expression of concern for canonical order and truth was met with immediate response. Formal conversations were held between representatives of the Patriarchate and the Church in America. However, for reasons about which it is only permissible to guess, the Patriarchate broke the negotiations. Since then, its representatives adopted a negative attitude towards all constructive initiatives aiming at Orthodox unity in America.

In the history of Orthodoxy in America, many opportunities have certainly been lost, but it is not by looking to

19

the past that order and unity can be restored. In the Encyclical published by Metropolitan Ireney on the occasion of his enthronement, the true path of our Church is clearly traced: "The way of our Church in America is her own and distinct way and she is, no doubt, to grow into one, native and local Orthodox Church. That which could be understood as temporary several decades ago has now become permanent and irreversible ... We believe the hour is coming when the free Russian Church will acknowledge and bless the way which God Himself imposed on us, the hour of peace and unity."

Meanwhile, in spite of all the difficulties, by the grace of God, the Church grows in strength. It does so because it is not *against* anybody, but *for* the only canonical and constructive future: one Orthodox Church, maintaining where necessary all national identities and traditions, in full communion of faith and love with the universal Orthodox Church, but one administratively and sacramentally. A decisive step towards that unity was the incorporation of the dynamic Romanian Episcopate into the Metropolia. The one Church of the future will not "Russify" the Romanians, or "Hellenize" the Church. It will secure a common life and witness to all without prejudice to what each national group has to bring to the common cause.

March, 1966

D CENTRE	SMV/1000	OPERATOIN DESCRIPTION	%

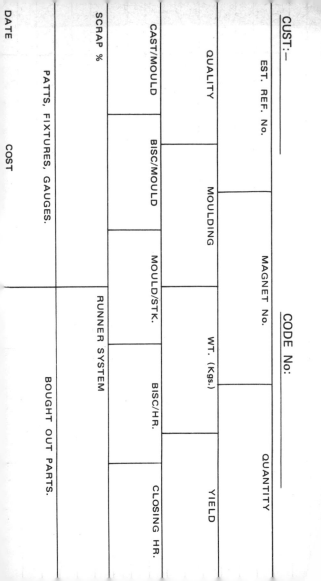

CUST:—   CODE No:

EST. REF. No.			MAGNET No.			QUANTITY
QUALITY		MOULDING	WT. (Kgs.)			YIELD
CAST/MOULD	BISC/MOULD	MOULD/STK.		BISC/HR.		CLOSING HR.
SCRAP %		RUNNER SYSTEM				
PATTS, FIXTURES, GAUGES.			BOUGHT OUT PARTS.			
DATE		COST				

Towards an American Orthodox Church

The Christmas letter addressed by His Eminence, Metropolitan Ireney to all the Orthodox Patriarchs and Heads of Autocephalous Churches is a great step forward towards the only possible future of Orthodoxy in America.

Its importance lies not only in the fact that it clearly describes the irregularities of the present situation, but that it also defines responsibilities. Whatever the mistakes committed by the Orthodox leadership in America, however strong and particularistic the feeling of the various national groups, the Orthodox Church in this country has received until now practically no help or constructive guidance from the "Mother Churches." Entangled in their own difficulties and struggle for survival, they were generally unable to look beyond and above the day-to-day advantages which their respective American branches were able to supply, and were blind to the fact that a canonically organized, united and strong Orthodox Church in America would be immensely more able to help them all. Of course, in many ways, their inaction in this respect was also due to direct government pressure aiming at restricting any really positive move on their part.

Recently, however, the Ecumenical Patriarch Athenagoras has publicly expressed his support for Orthodox unity in America in conformity with the earlier declaration of his predecessor, Meletios IV, quoted in Metropolitan Ireney's message. And the Moscow Patriarchate itself, in spite of its negativistic attitude towards any further progress of the Standing Conference, publicly approved the principle of Orthodox "unity" and "autocephaly" in America.

The "Mother Churches" and their representatives often

resent criticism of their actions (or inaction) by American Orthodox. They claim that they are totally free of government control or nationalistic purposes, that their aims are purely ecclesiastical and canonical. The brotherly and respectful letter of His Eminence, Metropolitan Ireney, gives them an opportunity to express that this is indeed the case, by showing a truly motherly concern for American Orthodoxy. Even if it is neither immediate nor direct, any help or blessing on their part will be received thankfully and enhance their moral prestige immensely.

Besides placing the problem of the Church in America on the agenda of a Pan-Orthodox discussion, the letter of His Eminence has a vital importance for the Metropolia itself. As the organic continuation of the great missionary work performed since 1794 on this continent, the Metropolia is given by its Primate the task of fully realizing its calling to become the American Church, together with all those who have no other goal than the progress of the Church as such, and of Orthodoxy as such.

This task must become the major point of the Agenda of the All-American Council (Sobor), forthcoming in 1967. Our Church in America possesses the blessed and God-given opportunity to speak and to act for the Truth itself. His Eminence, Metropolitan Ireney, has solemnly done so. It is now time for the entire Church to follow the voice of the Shepherd.

January, 1967

The Future of Our Church

One of the main features of the Sobor, forthcoming in November, is that it is being officially asked to discuss the future of the Church in America, not only theoretically but practically. And this orientation towards the future, the definition of a clear, canonical, unquestionable goal, is certainly much more constructive than discussions about the past or complaints about the present.

Who can deny that, among the Orthodox in America, there is a widespread consensus about the necessity of establishing a unified canonical structure, one Orthodox Church of America? However, the other ecclesiastical bodies and jurisdictions have *originally* defined their mission and purpose in national terms. The Metropolia has the exclusive privilege of having been established *originally* as an American Church. And today it is not committed, as others are, to protect or represent the interests of some distant Mother Church. This gives the Metropolia a unique freedom and a unique responsibility to serve and represent the mission of the Orthodox Church *in America,* and nowhere else.

However, as we have already stated repeatedly, the establishment of a canonically unified and autocephalous Orthodox Church in America would not mean forgetting the heritage and present plight of the Orthodox Church in Eastern Europe, and particularly in Russia; on the contrary, a strong Orthodoxy in America would be able to help the Mother Church much more efficiently. Neither would it mean a cheap and superficial "americanization": all the valid national peculiarities, languages and traditions can be easily safeguarded on the parochial or diocesan levels.

At the forthcoming Sobor, the Church will therefore be

given the opportunity to take a careful but decisive step forward in the spirit of the letter recently addressed by His Eminence, Metropolitan Ireney, to the Patriarchs and Heads of Autocephalous Churches. This step will be based neither on self-righteousness—for in the history of the Metropolia there were enough mistakes made and opportunities lost— nor on presumptuousness, for we are calling others not to "follow us," but to comply voluntarily and consciously with the age-long canonical tradition of the entire Orthodox Church, our common Mother, and to start to build American Orthodoxy all together.

June-July, 1967

The Way to the Future

By an overwhelming majority, the 13th All American Church Council (Sobor) has expressed itself in favor of the establishment of one Orthodox Church of America as the only possible and canonical solution of the present problem assailing the Church. This step has been taken not because anything of the "Russian" heritage is now to be discarded, not because the members of the Sobor forgot that the suffering Church of Russia needs today the strong support of those of her children who can speak freely, but because the Russian Church herself had laid the foundation of American Orthodoxy 173 years ago, and that this foundation of the Metropolia as the local, territorial, multinational, American Church is the only solid ground of its canonicity.

The majority which approved the reaffirmation of this principle was clearly ready to change immediately the official designation of our Church from its rather cumbersome present title—the Russian Orthodox Greek Catholic Church of America—to a more realistic and accurate—The Orthodox Church in the Americas. If this formal step was postponed until the next Sobor, scheduled to meet in two years, it was because more debate on the issue was considered prudent, especially with our Orthodox brothers of the other jurisdictions, without whom no final solution of the problem of Orthodox unity is possible.

Let us hope and pray that the forthcoming period of two years reflection will lead us all to the goal which the Sobor has considered as the only possible solution.

During its sessions, the Sobor had shown an unprecedented sense of responsibility and maturity in resolving many other thorny issues: the financial problem, Article VI of the Normal

25

Statute, the Calendar issue. This growing unity, based upon mutual trust and common dedication, gave to all a new sense of confidence in the future of the American Orthodox Church.

December, 1967

St Vladimir's: 30

The slow but sound development of Orthodox theological education in America is one of the most comforting achievements of our Church life. Without educated priests, the Church would not include today so many active and educated laymen. It would be unable to witness for its faith before the world and other Christians. It could not educate young people and answer the searching, critical mind of new, university-trained generations. It would not be in a position to interpret intelligently the inexhaustible richness of Scripture, the wisdom handed down to us by the Fathers, and to react creatively to the challenge of our own age.

Thus, when in 1937 the authorities of the Church and a dedicated group of laymen took the decision to reestablish in America a school of higher theological education, which required also, as did the theological schools of all other denominations, a college education, they took a decisive option. They considered that Orthodoxy in America had a permanent future, that it was not only an immigrant Church called to answer the requirements of another country and another age, but the true Church of God, true for ALL countries and ALL ages, including America in the twentieth century. In taking this option, they followed the example of all the responsible Church-builders of the past, including those who, yet in the last century, established theological schools in Alaska, in Minneapolis and in Tenafly.

In the same year other Orthodox centers for training clergy also saw the light of day in America: St Tikhon's pastoral school and the Greek Seminary in Pomfret, Conn. Since then both of these schools have had their own history and their own development. St Vladimir's, for its part,

27

achieved a graduate-degree granting privilege. It has a qualified faculty and sponsors numerous publications. This year it granted Honorary Doctorates of Theology to several well-known Orthodox theologians of the "old countries," thus witnessing to its unity with world Orthodoxy, its faithfulness to tradition and its conviction that Orthodoxy in America has reached maturity, that it qualifies for the status of becoming an independent, grown-up Church.

There is no reason for triumphalism, however. Our Church and our theological schools still have problems. The major problem is the lack of a system and coordination. Much of our means is lost through duplication, competition and mutual distrust. St Vladimir's, Holy Cross, St Tikhon's, Christ the Saviour—four schools for the training of Orthodox priests which should at least coordinate their programs in such a way so that our theological education may follow one single pattern. Competition, in the same Russian Metropolia, between St Tikhon's and St Vladimir's—competition for donors' money, for students, for influence—should be replaced by a common acceptance of one program of studies, clearly divided into undergraduate and graduate divisions, roughly corresponding to what "seminaries" (undergraduate schools) an "academies" (graduate schools) were in Russia. To achieve this is an obvious need. A similar reform has been accomplished, at least formally, at Holy Cross in Brookline.

For Holy Cross and St Vladimir's there is also no other constructive way to the future than closest cooperation, with the eventual aim of achieving a single American Orthodox Graduate union, qualified to grant all academic degrees.

These are the considerations which come to the mind of the writer in connection with the celebration of St Vladimir's thirtieth anniversary; for, obviously, St Vladimir's belongs to the whole of American Orthodoxy and its future is inseparable from the total progress of our faith in this land.

October, 1968

Standing Conference Takes Step

The approval by the recent special meeting of the Standing Conference of a firm appeal to canonical unity of the Orthodox jurisdictions in America is a positive step forward in the life of Orthodoxy.

The project is, of course, not new and its realization is long overdue. Archbishop Tikhon had officially presented it in 1906 in a report to the Russian Holy Synod, and the Ecumenical Patriarch Meletios became the proponent of a modified form of the same plan in 1922. (Texts published in St Vladimir's Seminary Quarterly, vol. 5, 1961.) Those who claim that administrative unity, preserving, where necessary, all the national identities and traditions, is not desirable, or that the Orthodox Church in America is not "ready" for it, do in fact oppose the entire canonical tradition of Orthodoxy, as well as the judgment of the best leaders of our Church in this country as expressed long ago. If unity was already taken for granted in 1906, the fact that it is not realized in 1968 is really shameful.

The Standing Conference appeal, which is echoed by the document recently prepared by "Syndesmos" is addressed to the Pre-Conciliar Pan-Orthodox Commission meeting this summer in Geneva, Switzerland (and not in Crete, as previously announced). It is a modest and respectful document, directed to the various "Mother Churches." There is no doubt that if the latter were able to deal with their pastoral and canonical responsibilities in America without nationalistic prejudice, in full freedom from governmental pressure and with full knowledge of the real situation, the solution—in the form of either an autonomous or an autocephalous Church—would be forthcoming soon. Unfortunately, the

29

Standing Conference is unable to modify the conditions in which the "Mother Churches" now live. It simply takes the responsibility for making them fully aware of the fact that some action is necessary and unavoidable. The vote of the Conference was not unanimous; but this does not make it less authoritative, for the opponents of the adopted resolution represent no more than two percent of the Orthodox parishes in America.

The responsibilities are now clearly taken and this in itself is great progress.

June-July, 1968

Towards Autocephaly

According to Orthodox tradition and canon law, Orthodox Christians living in any given country or territory must live as one Church, united locally and in full communion and cooperation with the Orthodox Churches of other parts of the world. In America this unity was a self-evident reality until 1922: a diocese established here in 1870 by the Russian Church welcomed into its fold all immigrant groups and guaranteed to all of them an orderly church life, as well as the possibility to preserve their individual national traditions.

In 1906 Archbishop Tikhon, then head of the diocese and later Patriarch of Moscow, suggested that the ever increasing numbers of Orthodox faithful, the particular conditions of American life and the multinational character of the American Church require an "autocephalous"—i.e., administratively independent—status for the Orthodox Church of America. The coming year may see the fulfillment of the late Patriarch's vision.

The history of Orthodoxy in America since 1906 is a history of tremendous growth but it is also a history of tragedy and division. Today we are beginning to see light at the end of the tunnel.

The establishment of an autocephalous "Orthodox Church of America" by the Patriarchate which first brought and organized Orthodoxy in America will solve the painful conflict between the Metropolia and its Mother Church. But it also will provide American Orthodoxy as a whole with a new and unquestionable opportunity. The existence in the same country of several parallel Orthodox jurisdictions—the Greek, the Russian, the Syrian, the Romanian, the Albanian, etc.—is a canonical abnormality which hampers the spiritual

31

and social witness of Orthodoxy. In the eyes of an outsider, we appear as a congregation of ethnic tribes. All must find their place in the one Orthodox Church of America.

Obviously, there can be no question of making this unity "under the Russians." Autocephaly implies the end of ecclesiastical colonialism: Church life in America must have no other goals than the progress of Orthodoxy in this country and the contribution to the progress of the faith everywhere. It cannot serve particular interests. But it can and must preserve and guarantee all national traditions: ethnic parishes will still use their own liturgical languages; dioceses will remain organized according to their existing statutes. This diversity in unity can remain for the decades to come. The Orthodox Church of America must be the Church of them all.

It is also obvious that the Patriarchate of Moscow could grant autocephaly only to those who asked for it. However, the canonical rights which it exercised before 1922 over all the Orthodox of America makes its present action relevant for them all. It would indeed be a blessing for the future of the Church if all existing jurisdictions could, jointly or separately, ask their respective Mother-Churches for a release and thus occupy in the one Orthodox Church of America the position to which their numbers and spiritual wealth entitles them! As we have repeatedly stated, the Mother Churches themselves could greatly benefit from a united American Orthodoxy.

December, 1969

Too Early or Too Late?

When the issue of a united Orthodox Church of America is raised, one of the standard reactions is that "we are yet immature" and that it is "too early" to speak of it.

However, Patriarch Tikhon spoke of it as an obvious canonical necessity in 1906. Patriarch Meletios of Constantinople envisaged it in 1922. Bishop Nikolai Velimirovich readily accepted the idea twenty years ago. None of them thought that Orthodox Americans were immature, or that a united Orthodox Church would jeopardize the legitimate and fruitful diversity which may continue to exist between Greek, Russian or Serbian parishes.

The other objection is that the demand for a canonically unified Church should come "from the people," that, in a matter of such importance, the hierarchy cannot impose its will, even concerning the canonical order of the Church, an area in which it is obviously competent and for which it is actually responsible. But even if the hierarchy desired to abdicate its responsibility on this point, it is quite clear that even outside the Metropolia, which clearly and consistently committed itself to be the American Church, a very vast majority of responsible Orthodox laity favors, or accepts, the idea of unity.

Let us, therefore, stop saying that the question is raised "too early." In fact, it can rather be said that we are at least fifty years late. Since the time when there was a canonically united Church (before 1922), Orthodox people became accustomed to the idea of nationalistic separateness. They often lost the feeling—which they undoubtedly had in the past—that in each country there can be only one Orthodox Church. And, in recent years, there seems even to be a resurgence of nationalism, accompanied by a proliferation of new jurisdictions.

What Orthodox Americans do expect today is a clear action from the top, from the Church of Russia which laid the foundation of Orthodoxy in America, from the Ecumenical Patriarchate which today has such a large jurisdiction in America, from the "Mother Churches" who established their separate jurisdictions here after the breakdown of the original united diocese. In order to be meaningful, this action must be authentically selfless, i.e., it should express concern for America and not for the particular interests of any one of the Mother Churches.

It has been said very often that each of the Mother Churches, and all of them together, can only gain—spiritually, and even materially—if they contribute, without reservations, to the creation of a united Orthodoxy in America.

May, 1968

An "American" Church

Eastern Orthodoxy, throughout its entire history, has been the religion of the people. With its liturgy using the vernacular, with its particular ability to assume the various cultures where it developed, with leaders who often assumed the responsibility for entire nations, Orthodoxy became inseparable from national consciousness itself. This is true for the Greeks, who like to identify Orthodoxy and Hellenism, for the Russians with their irrational messianism of "holy Russia," for the Serbs, who see no difference between pravoslavie and svetosavlje (the inheritance of St Sava).

The strength of these various forms of religious nationalism is tremendous: the Communists themselves are unable to deracinate it. This strength comes from the fact that Christianity has become rooted in society, in the family traditions, in the general world-view of entire nations: all this is an extraordinary achievement of an authentically Christian spirit, which assumes and transforms the whole of human life, and not only—as in our modern secularized civilization—an isolated corner of man's life. This wholeness of Christian life is what the great saints of the past have succeeded to build: the Greek Fathers of the Church, St Sergius in Russia, St Sava in Serbia.

But something quite new happened later, especially in the nineteenth century: the balance between religion and culture was lost. Instead of sanctifying their national life by submitting it to the higher ideals of the One Church—as the Greek Fathers, and St Sergius, and St Sava had done—the Orthodox began to use the Church as a tool for the perpetuation of their national, political or cultural interests. They began to think of themselves as "Greek Orthodox,"

"Russian Orthodox" or "Serbian Orthodox," as if these were
separate religious "denominations." Hence our disastrous
state of division here in America, where God brought us
all together.

St Paul had to face a similar situation in Corinth, where
Christians of Jewish background and Christians of pagan
background had created separate communities. He wrote to
them: "I appeal to you, brethren, by the name of our Lord
Jesus Christ, that all of you agree and that there be no
divisions among you ... What I mean is that each one of
you says, I belong to Paul, or I belong to Apollos, or I belong to Christ. Is Christ divided? Was Paul crucified for
you? Or were you baptized in the name of Paul?" (I Cor
1:10-13).

There is—in the One Orthodox Church—one Baptism, one
Eucharistic Liturgy, one Priesthood, one Faith. And of course,
there are many different people, whose identity—personal,
national, cultural—is perfectly legitimate, but only as long
as this identity does not divide the Church.

Today, fortunately, we envisage again our future in terms
of Orthodox unity. This unity existed—administratively and
canonically—before 1921, when all Orthodox of various national backgrounds were united in one single canonical Church
of America. No one ever said that their national identity was
suffering then in any way.

In restoring that unity again today, we will not create
a new "denomination," called "American Orthodox," but
we will all be one in the "Orthodox Church of America."
This Church will undoubtedly preserve, wherever necessary,
various liturgical languages and traditions, with all desirable
guarantees on the diocesan or parochial levels, and it will, of
course, welcome Americans, who do not desire to identify
themselves by any other national adjectives. The canons of
the Church actually ignore "national" churches: they only
require that in each area the essential Oneness of the Church
be visibly realized, so that our confession of faith in the
Creed—"I believe in One, Holy, Catholic and Apostolic
Church"—may not sound like empty words.

No one requires from us to cease to be what we are.

Diversity is not precluded by oneness. The future therefore is in an "Orthodox Church of America," where there will be room for Russians, Greeks, Serbians, Ukrainians, Arabs, Albanians and . . . Americans!

January, 1970

What Is Autocephaly?

In the universal Orthodox Church today there are four-teen "autocephalous" Churches: The Patriarchates of Constantinople, Alexandria, Antioch, Jerusalem, Moscow, Georgia, Serbia, Romania and Bulgaria; the autocephalous Archbishoprics of Cyprus, Greece and Albania, and the autocephalous Metropolitanates of Poland and Czechoslovakia. "Autocephaly" therefore is not expressed in the title of the primate (he can be called patriarch, metropolitan or archbishop, depending on local usage), but in the right of total administrative independence, officially recognized by all the Churches. The unity of the universal Church is expressed in a fellowship of faith and love, not in the power of one church over another.

Between the autocephalous churches there exists a hierarchy of honor, which is determined not by the respective number of their faithful, but by ancient canons and traditions. The Ecumenical Patriarchate of Constantinople, for example, even though the number of its faithful has been shrinking in recent years and is today reduced to a few thousands, still retains a primacy of honor granted to it by the ancient councils because Constantinople was then the capital of the Roman Empire and the real center of the Eastern Christian world for many centuries.

If, by the grace of God, the Orthodox Church of America occupies at last a position among the autocephalous churches, and even if, at the beginning, some of the Orthodox jurisdictions will prefer to retain their canonical allegiance to their ethnic Mother Churches beyond the seas, the Church of America will still be much larger in numbers and influence than several of the most ancient Patrtiarchates combined. It will be able to help them and also to express the voice of hundreds of thousands of Orthodox Americans in pan-Orthodox conferences. And, last but foremost, it will carry on the message of the Orthodox Christian faith in America, in full unity with Orthodox Catholic Churches throughout the world, dedicating itself fully to the only task which properly belongs to it: the building up of the Body of Christ in this countrty.

February, 1970

Towards Unity

The establishment in America of a canonically independent "autocephalous" Church can become a decisive step towards Orthodox unity, if the various existing Orthodox jurisdictions so desire. The fact that the Church of Russia—which was the first to establish a canonical diocese here in 1870 and which thus became the Mother Church of American Orthodoxy—is giving up its canonical rights and recognizes the Church of America as its Sister Church is a fact of tremendous importance to all.

No one can seriously question the canonical right of the Church of Russia to act as it does on its own canonical territory, especially since it is not claiming any further power or authority, but giving up its former rights here. A serious problem resides, however, in the fact that there are in America other national jurisdictions. Some of them—the Syrian-Antiochian and the Serbian particularly—were established with express permission of the Church of Russia, and the latter is certainly not entitled to dictate to them. Orthodox unity in America will come about if and when the individual jurisdictions will solicit their Mother Churches for a release and when this release is granted to them. The convention of the Syrian-Antiochian Archdiocese last summer already has passed a resolution urging American autocephaly: it would be illogical if it refrained from decisive action now. Actually, a joint commission already has been officially established by Metropolitan Ireney and Archbishop Philip to study measures to be taken.

However, it is very likely that some Patriarchates will prefer to maintain their jurisdiction over their branches in America, maintaining yet for a while an administrative pluralism on this continent. With them the autocephalous Church of America must maintain brotherly cooperation with the hope that gradually all the Churches will realize that the establishment of the only truly canonical order—one Church—is not only their moral and Christian duty, but is also in the best interests of Orthodoxy here, as well as of the various Mother Churches in the old world.

When and if all the Orthodox jurisdictions become seriously interested in organic unity, the status, organization and administration of the Orthodox Church of America may have to be readjusted. The "Great Council," which is now in preparation, may pass resolutions not only on America, but also on the rights and responsibilities of the old Patriarchates, and a totally new situation may then emerge. All this, however, may take time, while the situation of the Orthodox Church of America requires an urgent solution. The historic importance of the recent developments is that the Patriarchate of Moscow has acknowledged that a solution, acceptable to all, can be found only in giving to the American Orthodox themselves the right to administer their own affairs and in putting an official end—as far as the Russian Church is concerned—to ecclesiastical colonialism.

This is the only solution which would have been acceptable to the Metropolia. We hope that the coming months will see a free and creative consultation between the Orthodox Churches and the various groups in America, and that the Spirit of God—the only criterion of truth in the Church— will guide us all to unity, so that the very diversity of our traditions may enrich our common witness in the new world.

March, 1970

A New Beginning

The happy conclusion of the negotiations concerning autocephaly is not an end, but a beginning. For over half a century the history of Orthodoxy in America was continually marred by divisions, trials and conflict, and it was impossible to foresee an end to it all because none of the ancient Patriarchates seemed ready to take any action towards the establishment of canonical order. All the national churches having branches in America kept insisting on one thing: submission of their respective dioceses to their direct control. The result was not only the uncanonical co-existence of many jurisdictions on one territory, but also further schisms and divisions on political grounds. The latter were due to the fears—often justified—that the cooperation of several Mother Churches with Communist governments in Europe would lead to a limitation of freedom for their daughter churches in America.

What is really new and really constructive in the decision of the Patriarchate of Moscow is that it gives up its rights in America. To say that its action represents the imperialism of the "Third Rome," or a Russian blow against the Greeks, or a Communist plot, is simply ridiculous, and we should not lose time in denials or apologies.

For the first time the Church which established Orthodoxy in America and which exercised unquestionable territorial jurisdiction here until 1922 takes action in order to create in America a permanent canonical status.

We are convinced that all those who are able to think reasonably and objectively and to transcend pettiness or jealousy, will recognize that a new beginning has come for all. This applies, particularly, to the clergy and laity of the former Exarchate, who obviously have nothing to gain in isolation and resentment and whose future can only lie in the fold of the Autocephalous Church. The initial fears expressed by the leadership of the Greek Archdiocese have already been largely overcome, and if, still, Archbishop Iakovos speaks of "artificiality" in connection with auto-cephaly (New York Times, April 4), it is up to him to make it less "artificial" by contributing to a pan-Orthodox agreement which will lead to a full administrative unity in America. In any case the basis for such a unity has now been laid in conformity with history, the canons and the traditions of Orthodoxy.

April, 1970

Responsibility

The establishment of the "Autocephalous Church in America" is a significant event for world Orthodoxy today: it recognizes officially the fact that the Orthodox faith is not simply the faith of some ethnic groups in Eastern Europe and the Middle East, that its canonical structure is not bound forever to nostalgic reminiscences of Byzantium or Holy Russia, and that its mission is directed to the man of today and of tomorrow. We are not forgetting the past, for it is indeed the activity of the great missionaries of the past—Father Herman, Bishop Innocent Veniaminov, Archbishop Tikhon and many others—clergy and laity—which gives us today the canonical and moral right to autocephaly. But in the Church the past is always present and relevant: this is the secret and mystery of what true *living Tradition* is. The Church is *alive,* and its life is equally endangered if one cuts the roots of the past or if one refuses to recognize the responsibilities of the present. The forthcoming months and years will test our ability to live up to these responsibilities.

The Statutes of our Church give us ample opportunity to secure a fruitful cooperation between episcopate, clergy and laity on all levels of Church life. It is time for all of us to make full use of our rights and duties and stop arguing about petty and false issues.

To be "The Orthodox Church in America" means that our witness to Orthodoxy must transcend nationalism and be open to our tremendous missionary responsibility and to our responsibility for unity among ALL Orthodox Christians in this country, with the understanding that this unity will not be achieved by submitting one ethnic group to another, or by refusing to any group its share in building up a fully united Orthodoxy in America.

The status of autocephaly finally involves a direct role in shaping up the witness of Orthodoxy as a whole in the world today. This implies not only participation in formal pan-Orthodox conferences and, hopefully, Ecumenical councils, but also responsible and competent debating of contemporary theological, social and moral issues.

The situation of the Orthodox Church being what it is in Communist-dominated countries, in military-ruled Greece, in a fiercely embattled Middle East, the role of our Church could be decisive in making the message of Orthodoxy truly heard and understood.

These responsibilities are heavy: if the Church were a human organization only and not the true Body of Christ, they certainly could not be fulfilled. May the power of God "made perfect in weakness" (I Cor 9:9) help us.

May, 1970

Building

In many of our parishes there are building programs. We are building new churches, new schools, new homes. In the process, however, we should not forget that for us Christians stone or concrete buildings are only external signs of our true spiritual task: the task which St Paul calls "the building of the Body of Christ."

The establishment of the Orthodox Church in America as an autocephalous Church gives us a tremendous building task: we have to build churches, schools, missions, but, first of all, we must build an authentic and strong Orthodox consciousness in our clergy and our laity—the whole body of the Church—so that a true Orthodox witness may become a really dynamic presence in American society.

There are people who criticize us, but their criticism is exclusively negative and destructive; they do not want to take part in the building! None of them, so far, came out with a real constructive alternative, and, indeed, there is no alternative, at least in the canons and traditions of the Orthodox Church. There are those who say: "This autocephaly is a blow to the authority of the Ecumenical Patriarchate." We answer: "We recognize the honorary primacy of the Ecumenical Patriarchate, but so far it did not propose any positive way out from the canonical chaos in which we were living. If it takes an initiative which will be in accordance with the good of the Church in America, we will welcome it."

Others say: "This autocephaly, granted by the Patriarchate of Moscow, implies a surrender of our freedom to criticize the Communists." We answer: "Please read what the encyclical of our Bishops, announcing autocephaly, has to say about Communistic totalitarianism. Please listen to the broadcasts of the Voice of America, led by Archbishop John of San Francisco and other spokesmen of our Church. These broadcasts give hope to millions of persecuted Christians in the USSR. Please read our publications."

The same people maintain: "Patriarch Athenagoras, Archbishop Iakovos and the Moscow Patriarchate have betrayed Orthodoxy; we should stay away from them completely (and sympathize with Patriarch Athenagoras only when he attacks the autocephaly . . .)." We answer: "It is easy to condemn, but more difficult to maintain the positive message of Orthodoxy. We have been faithful to the latter. Please read our Bishops' encyclical on the Ecumenical Movement ("The Orthodox Church," May 1969) and their statement against intercommunion ("The Orthodox Church," April 1970). In the Ecumenical Movement we intend to maintain a truly Orthodox presence. We have criticized and will continue to criticize the relativists, including patriarchs and archbishops, but we do not want to overthrow all the patriarchates and all the archdioceses."

And so the dialogue goes. But is it really a dialogue? Is it not rather a deeper—and eternal—conflict between the Spirit of God, which always builds and edifies, and the destructive powers of evil? Let us be quite frank: those who criticize do NOT want Orthodox unity, do NOT want an American Church, and feel rather comfortable in the chaotic STATUS QUO. They try to justify either ecclesiastical colonialism or the existence of their own sect. We do not want to fight them at all because our unique interest is in building, not in destroying. We try to take St Paul seriously: "Love does not insist on its own way; it is not irritable or resentful; IT DOES NOT REJOICE IN WRONG, BUT REJOICES IN THE RIGHT . . ." (I Cor 13:5-6). We hope that they will do the same.

There is before us an immense task of building—a building of which Christ Himself is the "cornerstone."

June-July, 1970

Coming of Age

On October 20-22, at St Tikhon's Monastery, all the participants of the first Council of the autocephalous Orthodox Church in America felt that Orthodoxy in America has come of age. With an almost total unanimity, but also after free and responsible debate, the Council took two major and significant steps.

1. Following the decisions of the Synod of Bishops, which had fulfilled its canonical responsibility by leading our Church out of temporary self-government into the permanent and canonical status of an autocephalous Church, the Council exercised its prerogative of being the highest legislative body of the Church and officially adopted its new name: "The Orthodox Church in America."

2. The Council also adopted the text of a new Constitution, a short text defining the status and purposes of Church life in terms which leave the door wide open for the other Orthodox jurisdictions to join the autocephaly, according to proper canonical procedures. The Constitution will also serve as a guideline for a general revision of the Statute, or By-laws, which will be prepared by appropriate commissions, distributed to parishes, and, finally, presented for the approval of an extraordinary session of the Council to be convened in October 1971.

The spirit of unity, responsibility and ultimate seriousness with which these measures were taken give real credit to the bishops, clergy and laity: there seemed to be no trace of former misunderstandings and mutual distrust. Everyone understood that autocephaly is not only a major achievement, but also a task for the entire Church: the task of uniting all Orthodox Christians, the task of making them realize that the Church cannot be used as a tool for maintaining ethnic or political interests, the missionary task of bringing the Christian Gospel to those who ignore it, the task of proclaiming and practicing, in a true Orthodox way, the great Christian virtues of peace, justice and charity, with faith and hope.

If the Church truly becomes a living source of light, truth, justice and charity, no one will ever be able to challenge its claim to be truly the Orthodox Church in America.

November, 1970

Against Myths

During the last months, many comments of different kinds have appeared in the Orthodox press concerning the newly established autocephaly of the Orthodox Church in America. Much of the negative criticism has come from groups which have themselves abandoned the Orthodox concept of the Church, and discussion with them is useless. This is not the case, however, with the comments on autocephaly published by Andrew T. Kopan in the "Logos" (Vol. II, No. 9, Nov. 1970). Dr. Kopan is for Orthodox unity and against narrow nationalism, i.e., he espouses entirely the Orthodox concept of the Church which the Orthodox Church in America also tries to follow.

Our agreement with Andrew Kopan on the fundamental principles should, therefore, lead to an agreement in practice, provided one dispels the myths upon which he bases his criticism of the autocephaly.

The first myth to be dispelled is the one which purports that the Standing Conference of Bishops "was attempting to bring about the same thing," and that the Metropolia's negotiations with Moscow ruined this possibility. As a long-time member of the Study and Planning Commission of the Standing Conference, I can testify that at no time did the constituency of the Standing Conference even envisage the creation of an autocephalous Church in America. The only project which was repeatedly discussed was the project of a Synod under the jurisdiction of the Patriarchate of Constantinople, realized through pan-Orthodox agreement.

The project was supported by the Metropolia, not because the Metropolia denied the unique territorial rights of the Russian Church in America—it always recognized them—

but because it hoped that the American question, once raised on the pan-Orthodox level, would be solved with the agreement of the Russian Church. BUT THE PROJECT WAS REJECTED BY THE CONFERENCE.

It was then decided to appeal to the Pan-Orthodox Conference in Chambesy, Switzerland; but THE ECUMENICAL PATRIARCHATE REFUSED TO PLACE THE ISSUE ON THE AGENDA.

Meanwhile, in 1967 Metropolitan Ireney wrote a letter to all Orthodox patriarchs on the necessity of unity and later solicited an audience with the Ecumenical Patriarch himself. His request was supported by Archbishop Iakovos. The request was turned down (summer 1967) by a telegram. Unofficially, Istanbul let it be known that the Metropolia first would have to settle its canonical relations with Moscow. A little earlier, the Ecumenical Patriarchate had dissolved its Russian Exarchate in Western Europe, advising its bishops, clergy and laity to return to the Moscow jurisdiction. There cannot be any doubt, therefore, that Constantinople was fully supporting the claims of Moscow to exercise jurisdiction of all the "Russians" outside of Russia. It is, therefore, rather paradoxical to see Dr. Kopan objecting, in the name of the rights of Constantinople, against the Metropolia's negotiations with "the Communist-controlled Moscow Patriarchate." Constantinople always and consistently pushed the Metropolia towards these negotiations and opposed, with equal consistency, BOTH AMERICAN AUTOCEPHALY AND AMERICAN ORTHODOX UNITY, even under itself, because unity would, in fact, have implied a loosening of its administrative control over the Greek-American community.

The fact was, however, that the Metropolia did not want to go "under Moscow," that it could not be a "Russian" Church, because it was following the tradition of its founders, who at all times, until 1918, always worked for an American Church including the Orthodox of all backgrounds.

During the negotiations with Moscow, the Chairman and the Vice-Chairman of the Standing Conference were receiving detailed briefings; and nothing, at any time, was done secretly.

The myth of the autocephaly undermining the efforts of

the Standing Conference must therefore be fully dispelled.
The Standing Conference was facing a stalemate mainly because neither Istanbul nor the other "Mother Churches."
were desiring Orthodox unity in America. Now the situation
is drastically changed, the issue CANNOT be avoided any
more.

The main argument of Constantinople is that autocephalous churches are to be established by Ecumenical Councils. The argument is rather astonishing for anyone who
knows the history of the Orthodox Church, since the last
Ecumenical Council was in 787. But there it is—proposed by
the first see of Orthodoxy. The answer, acceptable to all, is
"Let us have an ecumenical council." Actually, such a council—an unquestionable authority for all—could not only settle
the problem of American Orthodoxy, but also revise the
order of precedence among the Orthodox world centers—
an order which was established at the time of Byzantium
and is highly inadequate today.

At the end of his article, Dr. Kopan proposes his own
plan for the future: an American Church, ruled by a Synod,
whose chairman would be confirmed by Constantinople.
This scheme is that of an autonomous—not an autocephalous—
church. As experience in the Standing Conference has shown,
it is highly doubtful that such a scheme would be acceptable
to anyone, especially in the light of the recent reactions of
Istanbul to the requests of the Greek Clergy-Laity Congress.
It is true that Dr. Kopan also proposes, in this case, to have
an American elected Ecumenical Patriarch so that the patriarchate would become an "American institution." Anyone
familiar with conditions in the Middle East, in Greece and in
the Balkans will recognize how fantastically mythological
such a plan is!

So, let us abandon myths and come down to reality. The
autocephalous Orthodox Church in America is here to stay.
It will eventually unite all those Orthodox Christians who
want to be simply Orthodox in America, with absolute freedom for all of them to preserve their languages, ethnic customs, practices, etc. There will also be for a time a number
of ethnic jurisdictions which will prefer to identify themselves

with their foreign connections. No one has the power to forbid them, and the autocephalous American Church has repeatedly pledged to respect their desires and the rights of their Mother Churches. All of them, however, can and must continue to cooperate through the Standing Conference.

Before the autocephaly the situation of all churches was uncanonical, because the canons formally exclude the existence of several jurisdictions on the same territory. Today the door is open for a restoration of canonicity. If the Ecumenical Patriarch wants to assume the role which should be his— to be the Convener, the Arbiter, the Center of conciliarity, let him exercise this role instead of appealing to non-existing rights! The autocephalous Orthodox Church will be the first to cooperate in any pan-Orthodox consultation on the future of Orthodoxy in America.

December, 1970

The Real Issue at Last!

For years there was much talk about Orthodox unity in America. The vast majority of the laity, as well as many young American-born priests in all jurisdictions, took this talk quite seriously and place their hopes and dreams in it. Now things have changed: the door for unity is open, but its former advocates are stalling, and some of them are even engaged in a frantic campaign of denigration, accusing the Orthodox Church in America of all sorts of crimes or criminal intentions.

Actually, the accusations fall apart by themselves. One cannot seriously maintain that the OCA is subvervient to Moscow, if one reads any one of the OCA publications. One cannot accuse it of overstepping the rights of others, when the Tomos of Autocephaly itself specifies that the rights of all other Orthodox Churches are to be respected, etc. In fact, all the denigrations have only one aim:

— maintaining a status quo which existed before April 1970, and which forbade Orthodox Americans to be simply Orthodox and American, but obliged them formally—if they wanted to be Orthodox—to become also Greek, Russian, Syrian or Ukrainian;

— a status quo which, in fact, admitted as normal the existence in the same place of several "churches," thus hiding the reality we all confess in the Creed: the "One, Holy, Catholic, and Apostolic Church";

— a status quo which made any real growth and mission impossible, submitting the various ethnic jurisdictions to the policies and interests of their ethnic centers abroad.

This divisive submission of American Orthodox to ethnic, or tribal, interests has powerful defendants. The most tragic element, in the present situation, is that the Patriarchate of Constantinople whose position as the "Ecumenical Patriarchate" obviously implies an obligation and a responsibility to stand above nationalism, became, in fact, the major sponsor of ethnic divisions. Fortunately, it is rather unlikely that Istanbul will persist in its present stand, a stance which isolates it from other Orthodox Churches, especially from the Patriarchate of Moscow, and hampers its ecumenical prestige.

In any case, the autocephaly of the Orthodox Church in America raises, at last, the real issue: Do we or do we not want to remain faithful to the mission of the Church of God in the whole world? Or is America excluded from the Church's mission? Is Orthodoxy forever to be bound to the culture and fate of Russians, Greeks, Romanians and Serbs? Since they already have their autocephalous churches, are the Americans to be excluded from that same privilege?

As has been pointed out on numerous occasions, the Orthodox Church in America has neither the moral right, nor the possibility, to force anyone to join it. It has also the intention—and obligation—to respect national identities in its own fold (the Romanian Episcopate, the numerous parishes who cherish their Russian or Carpatho-Russian heritage are witnesses of this). But what right do others have to prevent Americans from being Americans in their own country? What right does anyone have to prevent a free and canonical process of integration, involving parishes and groups who at present still preserve an ethnic character, but desire canonical order, according to which all Orthodox, independently of their nationality, must form one Church in a single territory?

These issues have now been raised and the process has begun. Any reasonable person can see that it is irreversible. How wonderful it would be, if those who feel unable as yet to cooperate actively with the unification of American Orthodoxy, would at least cultivate reason and charity!

June-July, 1971

The Forgotten Principle

One of the basic principles of Orthodox ecclesiastical organization is the unity of the Church in every place. Canonists call this the "territorial principle." In each town or periphery—whether small or big—there is one bishop who presides over one single community of clergy and laity. According to St Ignatius of Antioch (d. around 100 A.D.), he is called to represent God Himself in that community, which then becomes truly the "catholic church," i.e., the church which realizes locally the whole Body of Christ. This is why bishops are always consecrated for a particular place, i.e., a specific community of the Church. There are no "bishops in general," but only bishops of particular towns or areas.

The Orthodox Church has always preserved this "territorial principle" in its organization. When the Christians of Corinth organized separate groups for Jews and Greeks, who were reluctant to worship together and claimed to belong some to Cephas, some to Apollos, St Paul indignantly asked them: "Is Christ divided?" (II Cor 1:13). Similarly, as late as 1872, when the issue arose of creating two separate churches for the Greeks and the Bulgarians on the same territory of the Ottoman Empire, an inter-Orthodox Council, meeting in Constantinople condemned the very principle of such a division, labeling it as the heresy of "phyletism." (In Greek phyle means "race"; the heresy was in fact—"racism.")

For, indeed, a church based upon the ethnic or racial origin of its membership is a "heresy" (i.e., a "divisive group") because it practically suppresses two basic features of the Christian faith: the belief that in Chirst there is "no Jew, or Greek," and the commandment to bring the Gospel to "all creatures." A church which is restricted ethnically or racially cannot be missionary and, in fact, becomes a tool, serving the interests of its particular membership and not the Gospel of Christ.

In America the Orthodox Church, organized by the first Russian missionaries in Alaska and which later spread throughout the continent, has always defined itself in territorial and not in ethnic terms, welcoming everyone into its membership and always defining itself in missionary terms. By affirming this I do not deny individual inconsistencies and mistakes (for example, occasional appeals to Russian patriotism by some bishops, clergy or laymen); I only speak of the principle upon which the Church was organized. This principle was different from that which became the basis for the existence of the Greek Archdiocese, created in 1921 specifically for Americans of Greek background and using Greek as their liturgical language. (This legal requirement was abolished only in 1967.) Similar formal ethnic criteria were also accepted by several other jurisdictions which came into existence later.

As a result of this development, the Orthodox Church simply lost the very appearance of being the Catholic Church of Christ. It is being seen by all observers as a projection of various immigrant ethnic groups. And, what is even worse, the Orthodox themselves have lost sight of the "territorial principle" described above and have ceased to consider it as a norm of church organization. Whatever anybody says, the frantic opposition shown by some groups to the very principle of an autocephalous local church in America is indeed based on sheer ecclesiological heresy: the denial of what St Paul himself fought for in Corinth!

The arguments used are quite contradictory: one finds, for example, the same people accusing the OCA of not being "American" enough (its "bishops do not speak English," etc.) and for "forcing Americanization" upon ethnic groups! In fact, the issue lies not at all on that level: unity does not suppose "forced Americanization"; ethnic distinctions and traditions can (and must) be maintained in a united church (as they, in fact, are in the OCA: Russian, Ukrainian, Romanian, Albanian), but the Church must be One Church.

This is a matter of faith, of doctrine, of Divine Revelation about the new man in Christ. If this truth is maintained as an ultimate norm, pastoral accommodations, temporary arrangements and mutual agreements can give all necessary security to all linguistic and national groups, whether they choose to join the OCA or to remain dependent upon their Mother Churches abroad. We do constantly contradict the norms of Church life, in both our private lives and in actions as the Church. These contradictions are often nothing more than pastoral condescensions which ultimately serve the good of the Church. But they cannot have value or Christian significance unless the norms themselves are preserved as such and are kept in mind as the ultimate meaning of the Church's existence. Without these norms, the Church ceases to be the Church.

January, 1972

Where Do We Stand?
Hope from Constantinople?

More than two years have elapsed since the establishment of autocephaly. Several significant steps have been taken to achieve greater unity among the Orthodox in this country. After the Romanian episcopate, Albanians and Mexicans have joined the Orthodox Church in America. More importantly still, full eucharistic unity—not only in theory, but also in practice—now exists among those churches which are members of the Standing Conference of Bishops. In spite of some confrontations following the proclamation of the autocephaly, cooperation has never been broken between the major Orthodox jurisdictions in America.

The fact that not all are ready yet to define their Orthodox mission in terms of THIS country's needs, and prefer to preserve their former immigrant identification in terms of jurisdictional affiliation, was known from the beginning. The mission of the OCA is to leave the door open to the only canonical and ultimately inevitable solution: union of all Orthodox Americans in one Church.

There is also reason to believe that the venerable Orthodox patriarchates of the East which—through lack of information or of desire to understand—were so far reluctant to consider the American situation for what it really was—are beginning to realize the problem. In an important book just published on the history and significance of the Ecumenical Patriarchate, the Metropolitan of Sardis, Maximos, one of the most respected prelates of the Synod of Constantinople, strongly condemns "phyletism," i.e., the HERESY which allows the Orthodox Church to be divided jurisdic-

59

tionally along ethnic lines. There is nothing new in this condemnation, of course—only follows Orthodox canons—but it is good to hear it pronounced again, in 1972, by a respected hierarch of Constantinople, who also in his book denounces those who would think that the Ecumenical Patriarchate has any new "papal" pretensions. He defines the privileges of the patriarchate as a "service" of unity.

In a recent interview, the new Patriarch of Constantinople Demetrios expresses the wish of visiting America soon. We do not know, of course, whether this wish will be realized, but how welcome His Holiness would be in this country, if he were to fulfill here this "service of unity," standing above nationalities and "phyletism," and contributing to the building up of a united Orthodoxy!

December, 1972

The Standing Conference:
Past and Future

At its last May meeting, the Standing Conference of Orthodox Bishops decided to table the project of a new constitution and to maintain its present "ad hoc" status as an organ of practical cooperation and consultation between the various jurisdictions. The project of the new constitution was unacceptable to the OCA because it would have "frozen" and legitimatized a basically abnormal situation in which one Church—the Ecumenical Patriarchate of Constantinople—enjoys the privilege of five voting representatives (the Greek Archbishop, and the two Ukrainian, one Carpatho-Russian and one Albanian members), i.e., half of the total membership. Several of those voting members have an insignificantly small following among the faithful.

Archbishop Iakovos again showed his pastoral wisdom and responsibility, when he himself moved to postpone further discussion on the proposal.

The Standing Conference has now existed for twelve years. During those years, it has not only acted as a symbol of Orthodox unity, but has also sponsored joint educational programs, joint student work, joint dialogues with the non-Orthodox, and joint concern for the Orthodox chaplains in the Armed Forces. We consider all this as a significant achievement of the past years, and a proof that wide Orthodox consensus exists on these matters.

On the negative side, one should also recognize that the Standing Conference has failed to reach agreement on the canonical level. It is not itself a canonical body. The criterion of its membership is unclear and the majority is supporting the principle—which the OCA considers as uncanonical—that Orthodoxy in America should continue to be organized along ethnic lines, with dependence of each group upon its Mother Church abroad.

The OCA is quite concerned with preserving and developing the past achievements of the Conference. It respects the attitude of sister Churches, even if it disagrees with them, and it will continue to be represented in the Conference through one of its bishops, who will be responsible to His Beatitude and to the Holy Synod. It looks forward to a pan-Orthodox solution of our problems and believes that the Lord and only Head of the Holy Church will not deprive His Church of His Divine presence and guidance.

June-July, 1973

The Ukrainian Issue

Since the Autocephaly, granted to the Orthodox Church in America by its Mother Church on April 10, 1970, there has been a new beginning in the history of Orthodoxy in this country. Not that all the problems and conflicts were immediately solved, but a degree of clarity has appeared in the situation. Those Orthodox who wanted to define themselves in strictly ecclesiastical and canonical terms, without losing anything in their culture, but simply admitting that the Church, being the Church of God and not of men, is above ethnicity, now know where they belong; those, on the other hand, who considered ethnicity as the prevailing factor, could stay in the jurisdictions dependent upon ecclesiastical centers abroad. The process is still not completed, but it has clearly begun and will continue—hopefully without too much tension—until canonical order and unity finally prevail.

One major group, however, remains outside of this process of clarification. The really tragic history and difficult situation of our Ukrainian brothers deserve careful and fraternal attention on the part of all the Orthodox. They have no "Mother Church" abroad, and they generally abhor the very idea of submitting themselves to Moscow. However, they clearly represent an American ethnic gorup among others, without being in communion with the other Orthodox, because, in the confusion of the early twenties, the creators of Ukrainian ecclesistical independence committed the grave mistake (which most of them later privately regretted) of having bishops consecrated by priests. The defenders of this method of consecration generally refer to a poorly substantiated "Alexandrian" precedent, but they are known as "self-consecrated" ("samosviaty") among the Orthodox. In fact, their arguments are exactly those traditionally proposed by Protestants, particularly the Presbyterians, who insist on the supposed identity of the offices of "presbyter" (or "priest") and "bishop." However, our Ukrainian brothers also consistently affirm that they are Orthodox, that they accept the seven ecumenical councils, etc. But it is easy to show that the faith of the ecumenical councils presupposes that the apostolic succession is a succession of bishops, not priests! In fact, all the Ukrainian bishops now living were actually ordained by bishops, but they persist in maintaining the false doctrine of the "presbyteral" consecration as valid in emergency cases.

On the North American continent, the largest Ukrainian Orthodox group is in Canada. Its origins deserve to be considered with objectivity and historical accuracy. In 1918 and 1919, the Canadian Ukrainians (most of them converting from the "Unia") recognized the canonical legitimacy of the only then existing Orthodox jurisdiction, which was headed by Archbishop Alexander (Nemolovsky). They petitioned him to accept them as a distinct ethnic group under his jurisdiction, side by side with the Serbians, the Greeks, the Albanians, the Syrians and others, who, at that time, constituted one Church under the Russian Archbishop, with the plan of an autocephalous Church already in the making (since 1905-06). The All-American Sobor which met in Cleveland in 1919, having debated the Ukrainian question, formally decided to accept the Ukrainians of Canada as a separate ethnic group, with a measure of ecclesiastical self-government. Metropolitan Platon was personally instrumental in favoring the Ukrainian cause. However, Archbishop Alexander, after publicly confirming the Sobor's decision, retreated from it later and made it known to the Ukrainians that they were in fact Russians and that there was no basis for their ecclesiastical self-government. It is then that the Canadian Ukrainians began their search for a bishop elsewhere, finding first the Syrian Metropolitan Germanos (who was on a fund-raising tour of the new world) and finally accepting John Teodorovich—one of the "self-consecrated" bishops from the

Ukraine. Their later history is less relevant for us. Our duty is to care for the future.

It seems that early this year the Ecumenical Patriarch of Constantinople had indeed taken an as yet unpublished decision to accept Archbishop Mstislav, the head of the Ukrainian Church in the U.S., as an auxiliary bishop of the Greek Archbishop of America. Whether the issue of the "presbyteral" consecration was solved in principle is not known. This solution has the advantage of placing the U.S. Ukrainians in communion with Constantinople, but it clearly means the end of Ukrainian "autocephaly" and a new conflict with the Patriarchate of Moscow which had Archbishop Mstislav defrocked.* It does not solve the problem of the Canadians, who have been in the past very critical of Ukrainian-émigré politics—of which Archbishop Mstislav is part—and whose essential loyalty is to their Mother Church in Canada.

It seems to us that the time has come to think of a positive solution, in the framework of Orthodox canon law, for the restoration of a true Orthodox unity with our Ukrainian brothers. This unity obviously excludes their coming "under" anybody, but it also presupposes that they discreetly, but clearly, renounce the principle of "presbyteral" consecration of bishops, which canot be reconciled with Orthodoxy and its age-long tradition. They then should be recognized and proclaimed as the "Autocephalous Orthodox Church in Canada," with territorial jurisdiction on the vast spaces of our northern neighbor.

August-September, 1973

---

*The decision was never formally confirmed and may never have reached the "official" level.

The Church and Ethnicity

The problem of the relationship between ethnic allegiance and membership in the Church of Christ remains a vital one in the life of Orthodoxy both in America and in the rest of the world. It is a basically spiritual problem involving the very nature of the Orthodox Christian faith, not simply an issue of ecclesiastical politics.

Having universally accepted the principle of worshiping in the vernacular language of the various nations converted to the faith, the Orthodox Church has become "Russian" in Russia, "Serbian" in Serbia and "Japanese" in Japan. Indigeneity has given Orthodoxy the power to influence the various national cultures, to shape these cultures from within in accordance with the eternal values of the Kingdom of God. Now, even Communism is unable to uproot Orthodox Christianity from the consciousness of East European nations. And, certainly, the history of Orthodoxy in America shows that all East European and Mediterranean Orthodox immigrants saw in their Church a harbor of both religious and ethnic values.

However, the spiritual problem appears as soon as the Orthodox Church faces the issues of ecumenical witness, missionary expansion and Orthodox unity. It is indeed fortunate that the spiritual foundations of Orthodoxy in America, since the time of St Herman of Alaska, were laid in missionary terms: the Orthodox Church defined itself as a faith not only for Russians, but, first for the Aleuts, Eskimos and Indians, and then also for the multi-ethnic waves of immigrants who came later, and finally for all those who want to join it. It is on these same original terms that in 1970 the Russian Church granted autocephaly to the Orthodox Church in America. We must gratefully acknowledge this truly miraculous achievement!

As we have pointed out frequently, mission and unity do not imply abandonment of real ethnic cultural values, which must, on the contrary, be shared by all, but they do imply norms and priorities which recognize the universal goals of the One, Holy, Catholic and Apostolic Church as decisively overriding the interests of immigrant groups, the political purposes of ethnic "Mother Churches" beyond the seas and of the governments which control them, and the manipulations of émigré politicians.

Recognition of these unquestionable norms and priorities is not incompatible with pastoral concern for ethnic groups. For example, the recent and tremendous influx of Greek immigration in both Canada and the U.S. imposes inevitable responsibilities upon the Greek Archdiocese in terms of increasing Greek-language programs, but it would be a disaster either to deprive American-born generations from the possibility to pray in their own language (which is English), or to slow down the joint pan-Orthodox educational and missionary programs which were set up before the arrival of the new immigrant wave. An identical problem is faced by the Antiochian Archdiocese—in many ways, a pioneer in "Americanization"—which now accepts in its fold thousands of Palestinian refugees. It is also obvious that all ethnic groups could continue to serve their ethnic concerns in the framework of a canonically united Orthodoxy just as well—and probably even better.

In any case, in order to fulfill its mission, the Church, first and foremost, must be "the Church," i.e., be faithful to its own divinely established norms and criteria.

In 1872, in the midst of the most frightful and shameful ethnic strife between Greeks and Bulgarians, an Orthodox Council, meeting in Constantinople and presided over by Ecumenical Patriarch Anthimos VI, condemned the heresy of "phyletism," i.e., the acceptance of the ethnic principle as being the only decisive factor in Church organization. Conformity to that decision is a condition for our mission as Orthodox Christians in today's world.

Januarty, 1974

Orthodox Unity: Where Do We Stand?

His Beatitude, Metropolitan Ireney, in his Christmas Message, raised again the urgent question of Orthodox unity. On the other hand, the Council of the Orthodox Church in America, which will meet next November in Cleveland, Ohio, is called to discuss the theme of the Church as "Mission."

Clearly, Unity and Mission are two inseparable marks of the true Church of Christ: the Church is both "one" and "apostolic," i.e., missionary as we confess it in the Creed. No "jurisdiction" which limits itself by ethnic ties can be truly missionary, except in relation to the ethnic group with which it identifies itself. But then it ceases to be truly "catholic," since it places a limitation to its membership. The marks of the one, holy catholic and apostolic Church are inconceivable if local churches are isolated from each other; together, they define what the Church of Christ truly is and what all of us together are called to become.

Since the time when it became formally "The Orthodox Church in America" five years ago, our Church has received the full right and the absolute obligation to realize the mission of Orthodoxy in America in oneness and in catholicity, above all ethnic limitations. Without any unhealthy triumphalism, it can be said that significant progress was achieved already: the initial pattern for integrating national ethnic groups into a canonically unified structure was clearly defined (*cf.* the status of the Romanian, Albanian, Mexican and Alaskan dioceses in the OCA); younger American-born men have joined the priesthood and the episcopate; there was significant progress in theological education (including the establishment of a new pastoral school in Alaska) and publications; numerous new mission-parishes were inaugurated. All this was achieved in the name of *Orthodoxy itself,* not of any human institution or ethnic group.

We wish that the major ethnic jurisdictions in America—particularly the Greek and Antiochian Archdioceses—had made progress in the same direction or, at least, had made alternate proposals to the clear and unquestionable canonical position of the OCA. Of course, the Antiochian Archdiocese, at its several conventions held since 1970, has successively approved the principles that a united and *autocephalous* Church is the correct solution for the American Orthodox unity. In its 1974 convention, it had approved a resolution affirming that negotiations for administrative unification must start immediately. However, reasons for delaying any concrete action on these resolutions were also found, so that no concrete action has been taken so far. From the Greek side, proposals for talks were left unanswered by Constantinople and scepticism about the possibility—and even the desirability—of unity was frequently voiced in America. Concrete proposals for unity were labeled as "utopian." This scepticism, however, is clearly inconsistent with the well-known decision of the Patriarchate of Constantinople condemning "phyletism" (1872), i.e., the organization of the Church along ethnic lines, in the same geographic area. It is also inconsistent with the views expressed recently in a book on "The Ecumenical Patriarchate" by an eminent member of the Synod of Constantinople, Metropolitan Maximos of Sardis.

All this allows us to maintain a firm hope that in the coming years even the sceptics will agree that the Orthodox understanding of the Church offers no alternatives to unity. And if one labels unity a utopia, then Christian truth itself, the very *raison d'etre* of the Church's mission, is utopian also.

January, 1975

Ethnicity, Americanization
and Orthodox Unity

As every year, the sermons delivered on the occasion of the Sunday of Orthodoxy have emphasized everywhere—in 1976, as in the previous years—the need for Orthodox unity in America. The theme has become a part of the ritual. Listening to those sermons, or reading them, as they are subsequently published in various periodicals, it becomes apparent that the *real issue* is still seldom brought out. The preachers belonging to the Orthodox Church in America are generally quite cautious in avoiding any controversy that would hurt others. The representatives of the ethnic jurisdictions, which depend upon foreign patriarchates, are understandably occupied in justifying the present *status quo* of division—in explaining that administrative unity would be premature, or in finding such unrealistic alibis as to say that each ethnic group should "put its own house in order first" (i.e., presumably Carpatho-Russians with the Russians; Serbs with Serbs, etc.).

Nevertheless, the fact remains that the real issues remain clouded in misunderstanding, and it is obviously the responsibility of the OCA to work patiently and firmly to make these real issues clear.

For example: Unity does not imply automatic "Americanization." There is indeed place for ethnic traditions in American society—and certainly in the Church as well. However, the preservation of these traditions should not prevent the Church from being missionary towards those who do not belong to the traditionally Orthodox ethnic groups or from allowing younger generations to worship in their own tongue, which is English. So, the issue is that of priority and organization. We still need "ethnic" parishes, as well as purely mission-oriented American communities. And it is unavoidable that the latter will grow in number and in size.

It is curious that the OCA is being criticized by some as being still too "Russian," and by others as imposing "Americanization" upon its members! The fact is that both of these criticisms miss the point entirely. Orthodox unity in America can be achieved only by making place in the One Church for Bulgarians, Russians, Greeks, Serbs, Ukrainians, Arabs, Romanians—as well as Anglo-Saxons or Germans! And this is precisely what the OCA is attempting to do with appreciable success.

The real issue is that there must be a "uniting Church" which is based on the principle of supra-ethnic unity, i.e., on Orthodoxy itself, its canons, its true faith. As long as there exists only ethnic "jurisdictions" there is really no compelling reason for either uniting them or for the Church to be missionary. Autocephaly in 1970 has made a "uniting Church" a canonical reality in America. This has been indeed a "moment of truth" for all of us. Those who accuse the OCA of being "too Russian" are welcome to follow the example of the Albanians, Romanians and Mexicans who, without losing their identity, have entered it and are actively contributing in making it less exclusively "Russian."

In any case, no one—I say: *no one*—has come out with any concrete alternate solution for Orthodox unity in America, a solution which would be both in conformity with the canons of the Church and responding to the concrete realities of American society today.

June, 1976

Orthodox America, 1794-1976

All segments of American society take the opportunity offered by the Bicentennial Year for various forms of reminiscences and plans for the future. It is indeed remarkable that the Department of History and Archives of the Orthodox Church in America was able to produce, on this occasion, a book of such magnitude and wealth of information as *Orthodox America, 1794-1976.*

In the foreword the Editors apologize in advance for the "numerous deficiencies" of the book and for its "sometimes incomplete and sketchy character." These apologies, together with remarkable absence in the entire publication of any cheap triumphalism, make this publication a really serious piece of historical writing. For the first time all those who are concerned with one of the most significant events of Orthodox history in the Twentieth Century—the establishment in America of a really local and indigenous Orthodox Church—have the basic facts available to them in one single volume. One can only hope that the book will provoke others to the task of studying, collecting materials and correcting the inaccuracies.

But already in its present form, *Orthodox America* exhibits the qualities which future publications will also have to follow, if they are to be useful to their readers:

(1) It envisages Orthodox history in America as the history of the *Church,* and not as that of mutually exclusive ethnic groups. Orthodox unity is seen as the norm which had been accepted as the practical guideline by all Orthodox bishops in this country before 1921. It envisages the role of the Church and of its leaders in *guiding* the immigrant groups towards a proper Church order, not in providing a glamorous

leadership to the divisive ethnic tribalism which otherwise characterizes immigrant history.

(2) It does not try to "cover up" the mistakes of anyone, and least of all those of the Russian Church leadership, which was frequently inconsistent with its stated goals and failed to provide the needed leadership to parishes, to ethnic groups, to a confused, though often impassionately committed laity.

(3) It makes a serious and remarkably successful attempt at unveiling the inner problems of local communities, their aspirations, their hopes, their failures and their achievements. This aspect of the book is based on characteristic case studies, which was probably the only way of dealing with the problem in the framework of the book.

(4) It singles out those personalities who—like Archbishop Tikhon and all those who understood his sense of purpose and his intuition of what the Church is—patiently and humbly laid the foundation upon which we are now building.

The very fact that *Orthodox America, 1794-1976* could get off the presses is a sign of our Church's maturity, its readiness to face the truth about itself, its openness to the complicated problems involved in the growth of a multi-ethnic united Orthodoxy, its ability to recognize both the achievements and the errors of the past. All these are conditions for a healthy development in the future, if only God wills—and we know He does—that there be a mission for the Orthodox Church in this country.

February, 1976

Renewed Commitment

The election of Metropolitan Theodosius makes it inevitable for us to think once again of the present and future tasks of the autocephalous Orthodox Church in America, both in this country and in the context of world Orthodoxy.

We have often emphasized the two inseparable aspects of the commitment, which were renewed at the election in Montreal: *unity and mission.* Orthodox unity in this country remains the immediate and ultimate goal of our existence as an autocephalous Church, since all other jurisdictions— whatever the interest in Orthodox unity in America which some of their leaders, or members, share with us—also recognize other loyalties and priorities. The latter may be quite valuable in themselves but are obviously not conducive to canonical unity in this country. In any case, nobody has come out with a concrete plan or a proposal which would lead to Orthodox unity in America in a form other than an autocephalous Church. The Standing Conference of Orthodox Bishops (SCOBA), a consultative body, has never gone beyond some provisions for partial cooperation in practical fields and—if accepted as a permanent "model" of Orthodox unity—would in fact sanction a state of uncanonical division.

The need for true unity appears clearly whenever one considers the second essential commitment mentioned above: *mission.* A divided Church—or a loose federation of ethnic bodies—cannot really fulfill the apostolic, missionary witness of Orthodoxy. It is by keeping in mind the missionary task of the Church that one can best avoid dangerous substitutions, particularly the substitution of true unity in Christ with relative, or even false forms of unity, based on allegiance to

74

human values, however precious in themselves. The Orthodox faith, the belonging to the One Orthodox Church, requires that, in each place, there be one communion in the Eucharist, centered around one bishop who, in turn, is in unity of faith with the entire Orthodox episcopate in the world. The autocephalous Orthodox Church in America may not fully materialize this reality in its own framework yet, but it is formally committed to its principle, recognizing only concrete and temporary pastoral requirements which can best be handled through the wise application of ecclesiastical "economy."

So the establishment of the American Autocephaly in 1970 had laid the ground for true unity and for authentic mission. This act of the Church of Russia has been often misinterpreted, as if it was unilaterally pursuing selfish goals. The progress of the OCA in the past seven years and its record, as a fully independent Church, uniting and honoring many ethnic traditions and witnessing to the religious rights of persecuted Chirstians, is there to be evaluated by any impartial observer. In any case, our Church has become a permanent reality not only in America but in world Orthodoxy as well. Clearly, the final unification of Orthodoxy in this country will require a wide Orthodox agreement which hopefully will emerge in the framework of the "Great Council" now under preparation, but no resolution of the problems involved is possible outside of those permanent principles of Orthodox ecclesiology—one Church in every place—which form the rationale of our autocephaly.

The OCA, led by its new Primate, will certainly and gladly participate in the pan-Orthodox tasks lying ahead, but it will never accept that the permanent basis of its commitment to canonical order, unity and mission, be put in question.

November, 1977

Blind Phyletism

On February 27, 1977, the Sunday of Orthodoxy, a solemn concelebration of Orthodox hierarchs, members of the Standing Conference of Orthodox Bishops, took place at the Greek Cathedral in New York. Archbishop Philip Saliba, head of the Antiochian Archdiocese, was the speaker for the occasion. In his homily the Archbishop took up the familiar theme of Orthodox unity, developing ideas which he himself—and others—have repeatedly suggested in the past, including the possibility that all the Orthodox Churches, by common agreement, establish an Orthodox patriarchate in America.

The occasion would have been a useful but actually a rather routine celebration of Orthodox unity, if it had not provoked quite an extraordinary and well-orchestrated campaign in the Greek newspapers, both in the United States and in Greece, against Archbishop Philip and also against the Greek Archbishop Iakovos, who hosted the other hierarchs in his cathedral on the Sunday of Orthodoxy. The campaign, raging in newspapers like *Ethnikos Keryx* (New York), *Estia* (Athens) and *Kathemerine* (Athens), claimed that the idea of an independent patriarchate was "revolutionary," that "Mr. Saliba (!) infringed upon the rights of a Pan-Orthodox Council, that he represents "anti-Greek" circles, that the "Arab hierarch" is part of a conspiracy to detach the Orthodox of America from their Mother Churches and to "de-Hellenize" the Greeks. The same campaign is directed against Archbishop Iakovos, since he did not object to the arguments of Metropolitan Philip. He is accused also of being a party to the plot.

The ineptitude of the campaign, the total ignorance which it shows of the real needs of Orthodoxy in America and its total contempt for the Church of Christ, as such, could have been easily ignored. We thought it wise, however, to inform all those who do not read Greek newspapers about the real predicament under which the leaders of the Greek Church in this country are exercising their ministry. If they were to move in the direction of Orthodox unity, they would have to overcome a rather frightening journalistic and political demagoguery by people who consider the Orthodox Church as nothing more than an ethnic club, designed to serve the interests of nationalism and, in America, the dependence of the various ethnic churches upon ecclesiastico-political centers abroad.

The mentality represented by those people has been condemned as "heresy" by the Council of Constantinople of 1872, under the name of *phyletism*. The council defined *phyletism* (a Greek word which can be best translated as "tribalism") as "the formation of special national churches, each accepting all the members of its particular nation, excluding all aliens and governed exclusively by pastors of its own nation." The council proclaimed: "We renounce, censure and condemn phyletism, that is national discrimination, ethnic feuds, hatreds and dissensions within the Church of Christ as contrary to the teaching of the Gospel and the holy canons of our blessed fathers."

The official stand of the Ecumenical Patriarchate of Constantinople is, of course, to verbally uphold the decree of the Council of 1872. Such is also the stand of all responsible leaders of the Orthodox Church. But how to go about it in practice, without first liberating the Church from the fear of demagogical blackmail, and also from direct dependence upon foreign governments' interests and policies? There is no other way, no other method, no other solution than a patient, pastoral but firm reaffirmation of those principles—truly Orthodox, truly canonical—upon which our autocephalous Orthodox Church in America stands. Its progress in the past years shows that the heresy of phyletism is bound to rescind and that all those who really desire Orthodox unity—without losing anything which is precious and positive in their ethnic traditions—will join us in our common Orthodox witness to the world of today.

May, 1977

A Fifth Step

Upon the initiative of Metropolitan Philip, the head of the Antiochian Archdiocese of North America, a Bilateral Commission, studying measures leading to unity between the Archdiocese and the Orthodox Church in America, met four times since 1981. At the first meeting (March 3, 1981), the Commission recognized that both sides desire the establishment of one self-governing Orthodox Church in North America under the leadership of one synod of bishops. The second meeting (September 17, 1981) refined the plan of unity by describing possible ways as to how the future united Church could allow for the preservation of ties between the Patriarchate of Antioch and those who cherish it— and intend to continue doing so—as their Mother Church, while becoming an integral part of a united Church structure in America. The third meeting (April 2, 1982) discovered that further steps can be taken only within the framework of a practical agenda of cooperation. The search for such an agenda was formally approved by His Beatitude, Metropolitan Theodosius and His Eminence, Metropolitan Philip as they attended the fourth meeting of the Bilateral Commission (February 28, 1983).

The fifth step of the process is the conference held in New York on October 25-27, 1983.

The statement describing the conference speaks of "mutual trust, understanding, cooperation and enthusiastic willingness" to undertake joint work. These are strong and enthusiastic words, which, however, are still probably insufficient in describing the true *discoveries* made by the participants that many endeavors in various fields are complementary, that there is eagerness on both sides to serve together in One Church, that duplication and competition are childish and futile, that the Orthodox Church in America and the Antiochian Archdiocese already share an identical commitment to Orthodox progress and mission in America.

The Lord of the Church will undoubtedly lead us in His own way in the future, but the results achieved during the "fifth step" have given the participants enough courage, enough faith and a strong enough commitment to make them feel that the process leading to unity is irreversible.

December, 1983

Orthodoxy and Ethnicity

This issue of *The Orthodox Church* contains a revealing report, published by the Bureau of the Census, U.S. Department of Commerce, concerning the ways in which Americans identify themselves according to their ethnic backgrounds. Anton Ugolnik, on the other hand, discusses problems related to ethnicity in our parishes. Actually, the statistics published by the Department of Commerce—while obviously useful for the understanding of the American religious scene—cannot be used directly to evaluate the ethnic composition of the Orthodox community. If one can say, with every probability, that the 959,856 Americans who identify themselves as being of Greek ancestry, as well as the "Bulgarian" and "Serbian" groups are, at least by baptism, members of the Orthodox Church, the same cannot be said of the "Russian" group (2,781,432), which certainly includes many Jews and others. However, numerous representatives of the "Ukrainian," "Slovak" or "Slavic" groups are undoubtedly Orthodox, as well as the "Albanians," "Romanians" and the "Yugoslavians."

Be it as it may, in the year when our Orthodox Church in America had adopted the theme of "Church Growth" for its recent triennial council, it is proper to consider the problem of ethnicity, and the following points come to the mind of the present editorialist:

(1) There is no doubt that the adoption of the English language as the principal language of worship and teaching is the absolute condition of growth. Indeed, the overwhelming majority of those whose ancestry is neither English nor Irish, still speak English, and this includes not only the traditionally "Orthodox" groups, like the Greeks and the

Russians, but also the much more numerous Germans, Scandinavians and Italians.

(2) One should beware of the notion that simply by adopting English as the language of worship, a parish becomes automatically non-ethnic. Very often, traditions, manners, attitudes and family ties continue to be influenced by ethnicity. This is true not only of the Orthodox. Just look at the Irish-Catholic or Swedish-Lutheran parish on the next street . . .

(3) The influx of new immigrants from the Middle East, from the Soviet Union and from the East European countries, particularly Romania, requires the existence—and sometimes the creation—of new ethnic communities, using foreign languages in worship.

(4) The fact that our Church defines itself as the "Orthodox Church in America" does imply essentially one thing: that it seeks to be "the Church," open to all. It does not mean that all its communities automatically have to become non-ethnic, or that it is a church for Anglo Saxons only, or that it has to abandon all things Russian, Romanian or Albanian. The multi-ethnic reality of American society requires that many mansions be made available to many distinct groups, each of which must feel at home in the Church. However, in order to be "the Church," the Orthodox Church in America must be *a)* united canonically; *b)* committed to mission to all men. It is not ethnicity as such which is an evil, but the wrong and un-Orthodox attitude which places ethnicity above unity and limits the mission of Christ's Church to one ethnic group.

September, 1983

Canonizations

The Church does not "make new saints." The saints are recognized by the Lord Himself in His Kingdom. What the Church can do—with the guidance of the Holy Spirit—is to glorify and to solemnly honor those men and women who have pleased God and to call the faithful to ask for their intercession. Such a glorification is a liturgical, popular and ecclesiastical act. It is accomplished, not so much for the sake of the saints who are glorified—for nothing can be added to the glory which they already have in God—but for the sake of the people of God. Consequently, the spiritual authority and significance of a canonization depends very much upon who accomplishes it and where, why and how it is accomplished.

The unusual massive canonization, on November 1 by the "Russian Orthodox Church-in-exile" of Tsar Nicholas II and his family, together with the thousands of martyrs who died during the persecutions of the Church in Soviet Russia, has been rather widely publicized. It raises questions to which responsible churchmen—including this editorialist—cannot fail to give a response.

The first rather bewildering fact is that such an action—which concerns one of the greatest tragedies of contemporary history, involving, not only Russians, but all Orthodox and, indeed all mankind—is decided by a small splinter-group of the Russian Church, a group which, by its own choice, finds itself outside the sacramental and canonical communion of World Orthodoxy. The decision is made without consultation with anybody as a deliberate affirmation not only of the martyrs' sanctity, but also as a self-affirmation of the "Church-in-exile," as the only "remnant of true Orthodoxy." The act, therefore, implies unnecessary and deplorable divisiveness.

My second remark concerns the obviously controversial fact of the inclusion among the canonized Russian martyrs of the late Tsar and his family. Of course, one can hope that the eminently dignified, courageous and, indeed, Christian way in which the Emperor, the Empress, their children, together with a few faithful servants, accepted their fate has redeemed—in the eyes of God—the mistakes and terrible inadequacies of a tragic reign. However, the last tsar died not as a martyr of the faith, but together with millions of others, as a political victim of totalitarian revolutionaries. The deliberate confusion between religion and politics, church and nationalism, Christian faith and monarchic ideology, the romantic and unreal vision of the Russian past which characterized the "Russian Church-in-exile" since its inception in 1921, and which provoked so many divisions in the Russian Church, are obviously meant to be reaffirmed again in the canonization.

Thirdly, the issue of the martyrs themselves. Indeed, they were thousands. And we know so many of them by name: those who, like Metropolitan Benjamin of Petrograd, shot in 1922, avoided all politicking and made every effort to find a way of satisfying the legitimate demands of the new situation; those who, like Fr Paul Florensky, died in concentration camps, simply because they preferred their priesthood (or simply their faith) to the security of anonymous professionalism; those innumerable Russian Christians who confessed their faith in Christ—and only their faith—and died for it. The greatest lie of the Soviet government is to present them all as political reactionaries or defenders of the old regime. And this big lie can only find support in a canonization which groups together, without any distinction, the true martyrs of the faith and the political victims of the Revolution. Furthermore, this indiscriminate canonization may offer to the Soviets a helpful pretext to force upon the Patriarchate of Moscow a disavowal, which would deny once more the very existence of religious persecution, and therefore of martyrs, and thus further humiliate the Church.

It seems to me that a canonization accomplished in such conditions lacks the ecclesial, spiritual significance which any true glorification of newly recognized saints must possess. This is utterly deplorable because the true martyrs, who died for their faith in Russia, deserve to be recognized and glorified. Our task is to make such an authentic glorification possible by the entire Church—not by an isolated "jurisdiction"—in a discriminate and responsible way. Perhaps the Synod of Bishops of the Orthodox Church in America could initiate a responsible study of the question of how the veneration of those true martyrs can take place without any divisiveness and without usurping the legitimate right and duty of the entire Russian Church, when it receives the freedom to do so, to glorify those whose blood, even today, sustains the faith of millions, not only in Russia, but in the entire world.

January, 1982

Why Unity?

Talking recently to a friend who does not belong to a parish of the Orthodox Church in America but who reads Orthodox publications, I was asked: "Why do you people continue to be so insistent about administrative and canonical unity of Orthodox jurisdictions in America? Isn't the Orthodox Church already one in faith and sacraments? Why not be satisfied with this spiritual unity, be practical and settle, at least for now, with jurisdictional pluralism of ethnic jurisdictions?"

The call for passivity and benevolent tolerance, implied in my friend's questions, is extremely attractive. Why not, indeed, relax a bit and reconcile oneself with a few more decades of our present, divided status quo? The problem, however, is that the Christian Gospel is not a gospel of relaxation. And the Holy Fathers of the Church would not allow a reconciliation with any "heresy." Thus, St Symeon the New Theologian called "heretics" those who claimed that the commandments of the Gospel cannot be realized in this life, and that that realization must be postponed until afterlife.

But is Orthodox unity really a matter which involves the Gospel itself? Is the refusal of it really a "heresy"? I claim that it is, at least when the present dis-unity is presented as a settled norm.

Without even recalling once more the canons which forbid parallel jurisdictions, it is easy to remind ourselves of the principles which these canons are supposed to protect. These are, in particular:

— The missionary dimension of the Church: there is no way in which a church, which defines itself in restrictively

85

ethnic terms, can preach to "all nations"; the one Church should exist in each place, to call all people, with all their diversity, to unity in Christ.

— The Truth of Orthodoxy, since there is a clear danger that "jurisdictions," in their multiplicity, become in fact "denominations"; just like liberal Protestants, the Orthodox are beginning to join "the Church of their choice," rather than the One true Church.

Very often, on these pages, we have insisted on the fact that Orthodox unity in America does not presuppose the disappearance of ethnic identities through forced and artificial Americanization; that it can be introduced gradually with the first stage being a unity of the episcopate in a common synod (as already happens in the OCA); that unity alone would allow the clear unmasking of secularistic groups, claiming to be "Orthodox," but in fact self-established and self-proclaimed.

So, unity is not to be defined as an option, but as a norm, established in virtue of our faith itself. Let us not say that Orthodox norms are impossible to achieve!

As far as America is concerned, it is primarily up to the Orthodox Americans themselves to go back to the canonical and normal unity. And this unity cannot, obviously, be realized under the jurisdiction of a distant primate beyond the seas, as was the case before 1921. It must be realized locally. One would wish, of course, that Mother Churches—and particularly the Ecumenical Patriarchate—were of help. Unfortunately, their own local concerns and interests seems to dominate their attitude towards what they persist to call Orthodox "diaspora." The forthcoming meeting of the commission, preparing an eventual "Great and Holy Council," does not even have the issue on its agenda!

So the responsibility is primarily ours. Let us not escape from it.

May, 1982

Planning Ahead

The recent meeting of the Commission for the preparation of a forthcoming "Holy and Great" Council of World Orthodoxy in Chambesy, Switzerland, has clearly shown that little is to be expected in the near future in terms of solving the problems of American Orthodoxy on the level of the Mother Churches. The issues on the agenda were actually either non-issues (discipline of fasting, monasticism of bishops, marriage problems) or problems needing further preparation on the level of the laity (date of Pascha). The Commission practically tabled all these issues, and did well: no changes were urgently needed in those areas and, even if it wanted to make suggestions, the Commission had no moral authority to make them.

But what about the real issues? Since 1970, when the Church of Russia established the American autocephaly, the critics of that action—primarily the Greek-speaking churches—are saying that canonical problems of that nature should be solved by ecumenical councils. There could not be any objection against that: ecumenical councils are, indeed, the highest authority in Orthodoxy. Furthermore, several Orthodox churches, e.g., the churches of Alexandria, Russia, Romania and Finland, have expressed their official views on the subject. However, no action has been taken for further discussion and for preparing the decision of an eventual council.

How else can solutions be found except through conciliarity? Unfortunately, the issue of canonical order, which is being violated by the existence of parallel jurisdictions in this country, was avoided at Chambesy. Furthermore, it has not even been placed on the agenda of the next meeting.

How else are we to react, except by admitting that the solution of the problem is not really desired by the Ecumenical Patriarchate, which is in charge of organizing the meetings? But the stalemate does not suppress the urgency of the issue. No formula has been offered, except that of an autocephalous church, governed by a synod of bishops adequately representing various national and ecclesiastical traditions. This is the formula already used within the Autocephalous Orthodox Church in America. It has been formally recognized by three patriarchates (Russia, Georgia, Bulgaria) and two autocephalous churches (Poland, Czechoslovakia). It is also *de facto* recognized by the patriarchates of Antioch, Serbia and Romania, which are in full eucharistic communion with all the Greek-speaking churches.

It faces only one psychological danger: that of acquiring a sense of self-sufficiency, of forgetting its task of uniting—freely, without forcing anyone—all the Orthodox living in this country and maintaining such conditions of internal pluralism, tolerance and "catholic" understanding which would make unity possible with those who are not yet part of it.

If there is any other practical solution for Orthodox unity, we would gladly hear about it. We are open to all possible and canonical suggestions.

December, 1982

Voices of Reason in the Greek Church

It is highly unfortunate that among those who are concerned with and committed to the idea of Orthodox unity in America the Greek Orthodox Church (both here and abroad) is viewed with increasing disappointment, sometimes verging on irritation. In some circles of the Orthodox Church in America (and the Antiochian Archdiocese), it becomes almost impossible to mention "the Greeks" without provoking remarks of despair about future common action and canonical unity.

This situation is unfortunate because it is often based on partial and superficial knowledge of the facts, and reflects a lack of that forgiving charity which is the very condition of authentic Church life.

Indeed, on the local level, active contributions to Orthodox unity have recently become more noticeable, as is shown by the widespread involvement of local Greek bishops and clergy in common celebrations of the Triumph of Orthodoxy. Furthermore, voices of reason have been heard in several quarters. As reported by *The Hellenic Chronicle*, Fr Leonidas Contos, delivering the 1981 Patriarch Athenagoras Lectures at Hellenic College, Brookline, Massachusetts, spoke of "crisis" in the Church, and of the Ecumenical Patriarchate being the "hostage of crumbling buildings" (in Istanbul), with "its freedom to function choked off, its strength sapped, its influence diminished, its institutions shut down." However, Fr Contos does not suggest to break up with the "historical continuity" represented by the patriarchate, but to restore it "as an international and supra-national center" outside of Istanbul. Several influential and respected Greek Americans have voiced similar concerns recently. Furthermore, in the same lectures, Fr Contos questions the very concept of *diaspora,* or "dispersion," as applied to America, where the members of faithful are so much greater (in the case of Greeks) than that of their "Mother Church." Under such conditions, dependence upon the latter can only be "spiritual," says Fr Contos.

Interestingly, the same view of the *diaspora* is upheld in a recent article (which otherwise contains rather objectionable statements) by the new Greek Archbishop in England, Methodios. The archbishop agrees with Fr Contos that "we are no longer in any literal sense an Eastern Church." Indeed, Orthodoxy is either universal or it is not "Orthodoxy." In any case, it cannot be identified with "centers" and "empires" which have ceased to exist centuries ago.

How easy it would be, on that basis, to find a common solution to our problem: canonical unity in America, in "spiritual" and "unbreakable" communion with all the "Mother Churches"!

It is therefore quite wrong to concentrate one's attention (and one's criticisms) on the "system" which maintains the present *status quo* in the Greek Church. The inadequacies of that system become more and more obvious to the Greeks themselves, which partially explains the "system's" defensiveness, its constant appeal to the media, the desire to "look good" in the eyes of the public. Most frequently, such self-conscious efforts produce the opposite effect. Thus, for instance, the obviously uncanonical marriage solemnly performed during Great Lent, with widespread media coverage, between New York Governor Carey and Mrs. Gouletas embarrassed all the Orthodox, encouraged Greek Old-Calendarist schismatics and placed the Greek Archdiocese in a very awkward situation *vis-à-vis* the Roman Catholics. Similarly, commendable efforts at obtaining national TV coverage of Orthodoxy repeatedly produced the public image of a Church using incomprehensible rites in Greek—foreign, irrelevant and pompous.

Regardless of the "system," however, Greek Orthodoxy today is neither dead nor totally leaderless. In the midst of a largely secularized society in Greece, a hopeful revival of traditional Orthodoxy is taking place among the young. The monasteries of Mount Athos are being repopulated with educated and zealous young monks. Theologians like Chrestos Yannaras and John D. Zizioulas are among the very best in Orthodoxy today. In America, both by their numbers and by the quality of many among its clergy and laity, the Greek Orthodox community deserves a position of leadership. Finally, World Orthodoxy needs the Ecumenical Patriarchate as a vehicle of conciliarity and a coordinator of pan-Orthodox action, provided it becomes, as Fr Contos suggests, a truly international center.

Of course, the task of realizing Orthodox unity (as required by the canons of the Church) and the mission to all Americans regardless of ethnic background (as required by the Gospel itself) cannot wait for changes occurring in Istanbul, Turkey. This task and this mission have been assumed by the autocephalous Orthodox Church in America, in accordance with the inalienable and irreversible legacy of St Herman, St Innocent and Patriarch Tikhon. But it would be a spiritual mistake to settle for a new form of American sectarianism. If misunderstanding, passivity and negativism have characterized the official reactions of Greek-speaking churches towards the Church in America in the past decade, we have no right to despair and to exclude hope for the future.

June, 1981

Let Orthodoxy Come First

This year again, as Orthodox Christians gather on March 15, the Sunday of Orthodoxy, to celebrate a solemn service of Vespers together, there will be talk about Orthodox unity in America as a canonical norm, as a desired goal, or, at least, as a distant hope. And again we will realize that this unity is not coming into being because other concerns than the interests of the Church itself continue to prevail in determining the attitudes and policies of the various ethnic "jurisdictions."

First of all, there are, of course, the various ecclesiastical centers in the "old countries" who are unwilling, or unable, to liberate themselves from direct control by their governments. These governments are using the Church to preserve some influence upon ethnic groups in America. But there are also the wounds of the historical past which are being carried over into our ecclesiastical life, as many people fail to realize that past conflicts have outlived their significance.

The last situation particularly concerns our Ukrainian Orthodox brothers and sisters. I am mentioning them here because the All-American Council, meeting in Detroit last November, unanimously passed a resolution—moved spontaneously from the floor—calling the Autocephalous Church in America to contribute, as soon as possible, to a solution of their particular canonical problem.

In their case, the "ancient wounds" go back to the time when a bitter and often confused struggle for national and political identity in Galicia and Carpathian Rus'—controlled by Austria, Hungary and, later, Poland—deeply involved religion and the Church. The movement towards Orthodoxy (and away from the Unia) identified itself with Russia and the Russian Church, from which it was receiving moral and material help. This movement continued in America, and many of its leaders—or their children—are still among us. They naturally tend to see "Ukrainian" nationalism as a betrayal of Orthodoxy itself. However, the existence of the Ukrainian culture and nationhood has nowadays lost its religious dimension: the vast majority of Ukrainians today are Orthodox Christians (if they are not atheists). Furthermore, in America—and particularly in Canada—a very great number of Orthodox parishes prefer to identify themselves as Ukrainian.

In the early twenties, the Orthodox Church in America, headed by Metropolitan Platon, expressed readiness to recognize its Canadian Ukrainian branch side by side with other ethnic groups. The fact that it eventually backed away from that position was partially responsible for the tragic connection established by the Canadian and American Ukrainians with the "self-consecrated" schism (the practice of priests ordaining bishops), which placed them beyond the borders of canonical Orthodoxy.

To recall this tragic history today is to realize its futility for the present and the future of Orthodoxy in America. Orthodox unity simply cannot be realized unless all the parties concerned recognize their past limitations and mistakes, and resolutely begin to build the future together. As we have so often said, unity presents no threat to ethnic cultures, provided *Orthodoxy comes first.* But there is simply no way in which Orthodoxy can survive, and prosper, and develop, and pursue its missionary expansion, unless it is united in one Church, where no nationality or group has any particular privilege. How wonderful it would be, if we could suddenly realize that in America there is no Austrian, or Tsarist, or Soviet police at work to suppress our liberties, and that if some of the Orthodox jurisdictions are controlled by foreign officials (or émigré politicians), that this occurs exclusively by their own (regrettable) volition!

February, 1981

What Future?

"Orthodoxy, America and the future" will be the main theme of the forthcoming All-American Council, which will meet in Detroit, November 10-14 of this year. Indeed, for us Orthodox Christians these three concepts are inseparable: We are Orthodox, we are in America, as Americans—not as foreigners with a foreign religion—and we intend to stay in America permanently. At least, this is the meaning of the Autocephaly which we received ten years ago as the fulfillment of the expectations nourished by the first Orthodox missionaries: St Herman, St Innocent and many others.

Obviously, the future depends on God, on the Holy Spirit without Whom the Church would not be the Church, but a human organization. However, God has chosen us to be His co-workers. He has entrusted us with His mission in the world. With His help and in His presence, we are called to exercise our freedom to build, to create, to be "good stewards of God's varied grace" (I Peter 4:10).

The All-American Council meets so that our entire Church may act as a single body, facing common problems and transcending local concerns and particular interests.

If we really want to secure the future of our Church, we should be concerned

— with *Orthodox unity,* because we want the Church to be faithful to itself, as Christ's Body, and not as a projection of ethnic particularism;

— with *theological education,* which would provide the Church with leadership (and, on this point, the concern should now switch to quality, rather than quantity, because the shortage of priests is partially overcome);

— with *mission,* because time is rapidly passing when

Orthodoxy survived only through family ties: eighty percent of the marriages celebrated in our churches are "mixed" marriages. Belonging to the Church is obviously becoming a matter of personal choice; and, of course, we must welcome all those who discover Orthodoxy as the true faith;

— with *financial* resources, which, in our Church, are frightfully insufficient, revealing, on the part of most of us, a lack of responsible care for the progress of our faith.

On all these points—and many others—the Council will hear reports and take appropriate decisions. No aspect of the life of the Church will be excluded from the Council's concern.

Every delegate will be able to ask questions, receive information, voice opinions and make proposals. There will be committees and workshops, as well as plenary sessions, in order to give everyone an opportunity. There will also be common prayer and common participation in the sacraments of the Church.

The future will be in God's hands—and also in ours.

July, 1980

Orthodoxy, America and the Future

The Sixth All-American Council, scheduled to meet in Detroit, Michigan next November, should be an occasion for reflection and new commitment. "Orthodoxy, America and the Future" has been chosen as the main theme, which essentially proclaims that our Church remains faithful to its past, lives in the present and plans for the future. Indeed, the Orthodox faith is the apostolic faith: it does not change because Christ remains always the same and brings the same eternal life to all men at all times. To that faith we remain faithful, as did our fathers in the past.

However, faithfulness would only mean dead conservatism, if we did not apply that same faith, as a living faith, to the present—our American present. If our faith has been given to us by God, so is our existence in the present age also a gift of our Creator. It would be a betrayal of our past, if we were to forget our duty and our mission to our society, to our brothers and sisters, to our neighbors—in the present.

Sociologists of American religion have frequently observed that immigrants coming to the New World are quick to adopt the external features of American life and learn the ways leading to success, but that the same immigrants also tend to use their churches, or denominations, as tools preserving their original identities.

The analysis—certainly applicable to the Orthodox—must be taken very seriously by us all. It helps to understand the emergence of what is called "denominationalism." Each church or religious group is defined not so much by its beliefs, or theology, but by the particular make-up of its membership. One attends "the church of one's choice," or of "one's background." Credal obligations are reduced to a minimum and, very often, one looks elsewhere than in church for answers to serious religious questions. Gradually, the church becomes a vestige of the past, good for old people, or for some "ethnic fanatics."

Ten years ago, the establishment of American autocephaly implied our rejection of "denominationalism." We— as Orthodoxy has always done in the past—declared that we wanted to be "the Church" and not a "denomination." This did not mean that we rejected our "roots," but it meant that we recognized the Church as a divine, and not a human, institution, which belongs to God, and not to man. In the Church, there is place for all, whatever their origin, whatever their human roots, precisely because it belongs to God alone. Parishes—or even entire dioceses—may not be ready yet to define themselves as simply "Orthodox," but still feel the need to affirm their origins. Nevertheless, the Church as a whole cannot have a fully legitimate, fully canonical existence, if it wants to add different and human adjectives to the definition of the Creed: "One, Holy, Catholic and Apostolic," and if it recognizes other loyalties and other missions than the salvation of all men.

Certainly, the "Orthodox Church in America" is yet far from being, in its empirical everyday existence, fully adequate to its calling. But its self-definition is indeed adequate. We will have to "relive" that anew, as we meet in Detroit.

June, 1980

American Autocephaly
1970-1980

It is sometimes difficult to imagine that ten years have already passed since the historic day, April 13, 1970, when the patriarch and the entire episcopate of the Russian Church signed the document granting autocephaly to the Church in America. Indeed, that day was historic, since it saw the formal acknowledgment of American Orthodoxy, which had been involved in mission work in the New World since 1917. The acknowledgment came rather late. A *de facto* independence had existed since the early 20s. Nevertheless, it represented a tremendous step forward, especially by setting up a clear basis for Orthodox unity in this country and by terminating a painful canonical conflict with the Mother Church.

The newest autocephalous Church of the Orthodox world was now invested with a double task: (1) Making the Orthodox faith accessible to all Americans, not as a foreign import—"Russian," a "Greek," or a "Serbian," ethnic church—but as the truly Catholic and Apostolic faith; (2) Offering a canonical framework for Orthodox unity, without suppressing the wealth of legitimate pluralism of liturgical languages, traditions and customs which reflect the reality of Orthodoxy in America today.

Was this task fulfilled? One can answer this question by referring to facts which point to clear and substantial progress. Of the thirteen active bishops of the Orthodox Church in America today, five—including the Head of the Church, His Beatitude, Metropolitan Theodosius—are American born. If one considers the same episcopate of our

Church in terms of its ability to realize Orthodox unity, one can notice that it includes bishops not only of native American, or Russian backgrounds, but also one Romanian, one Bulgarian, one Frenchman and one Mexican. The unity which exists among them is not symbolic, but real: it is embodied in the regular work of the Holy Synod. What gives reality to their unique commitment is Orthodoxy only, and no other ethnic or political pursuit. This image of concord, which does not exist anywhere else in the Orthodox world today, shows that canonical unity *is possible,* that it does not imply the supremacy of one ethnic group over another.

Of course, the record of the past ten years also includes disappointments, and particularly the tenacious insistance of some groups to remain in the administrative dependence of Mother Churches beyond the seas and the equal tenacity of the same Mother Churches in practicing ecclesiastical colonialism in America. However, even in these cases there is progress: everyone seems to admit that unity is canonically necessary and practically desirable. The problem is only in finding the way of putting the canons into practice. And since no one has offered any practical solution, except the solution which the OCA offers since 1970, one can only hope that the next decade will alleviate the fears, dispel the suspicions and bring about that unity of which St Paul wrote: "By one Spirit we were all baptized into one body—Jews and Greeks, slaves or free—and all were made to drink of one Spirit" (I Cor 12:13).

April, 1980

A Free Debate on Orthodox Unity

By common agreement, the issue of overlapping jurisdictions in many countries, including America particularly,
stands at the center of the agenda for a "Great Council" of
the world Orthodox Church. There is a unanimous consensus of principle that such a jurisdictional pluralism is
canonically wrong. It reflects division, whereas the structure
of the Church should express unity.

We are publishing large excerpts from a statement by
the Archbishop of Carelia and all Finland, Paul, which
reports on the state of the discussion presently taking place
on the practical ways of securing Orthodox canonical unity
in the lands of what is usually called the "diaspora."

In preparation for the future Council, five Churches
committed themselves to write reports on the issue. These
were the Churches of Constantinople, Antioch, Russia,
Romania and Greece. Already two years ago, the reports
from Antioch, Russia and Romania were received at the
Secretariate, established in Chambesy, Switzerland. No reports from Constantinople or Greece were available, but the
Greek Patriarchate of Alexandria submitted one on its
own initiative.

The essence of these reports is the following:

• Antioch fully supports the establishment of new autocephalous (independent) Orthodox churches and thus considers that administrative independence is the road to unity.

• Romania places much more emphasis on the ethnic ties
between "Mother Churches" and their foreign branches, but
also admits that autocephaly should be the goal for those
"new" churches which are the results of missionary work
of the existing churches.

100

• The Church of Russia presents detailed and practical proposals for the solution of the canonical problem in America; it suggests that Constantinople grant autocephaly to the Greek Archdiocese, so that Orthodox Greek Americans may receive the possibility of reaching agreement on unity with the already existing autocephalous Orthodox Church in America by themselves.

• The Patriarchate of Alexandria alone supports the theory that all Orthodox Christians of all ethnic backgrounds should accept the jurisdiction of Constantinople, because they live in "barbarian," i.e., non-Greek-speaking lands.

Archbishop Paul himself is a respected member of the hierarchy of the Patriarchate of Constantinople. His strong critique of the "Greek" approach—which he considers as the main obstacle to a pan-Orthodox agreement—is all the more significant. He suggests that Constantinople should turn over the jurisdictional rights over the Greek "diaspora" to the autocephalous Church of Greece. Such an "act of humility" would strengthen the prestige of the Ecumenical Patriarchate as a truly pan-Orthodox center standing above nationalities, and redress the present situation which practically makes it into a "Greek" patriarchate with unreasonable claims over other ethnic groups.

Whether or not one agrees with his suggestions, one should congratulate Archbishop Paul for opening up a free discussion of the existing problems. The Archbishop is an honest and courageous hierarch. He is also a free man and a Westerner who has only a limited patience for Byzantine secrecy and the oppressing atmosphere of fear and suspicion which, for external reasons, dominate the life of many of the Orthodox "Mother Churches." At the end of his statement, he voices legitimate indignation that so far no commission and no other channel of discussion was established to discuss the matter of the reports. This delay makes him doubt that there is a real intention in Constantinople to hold a council at all, since the majority of Orthodox Churches is clearly against the recognition of Constantinople's rights over the "barbarians."

Whatever future there is for the council idea on the

world level, Archbishop Paul certainly asks the right questions. One can only add a point which was often made in this column: the issue of Orthodox unity in America cannot and will not be solved without the Orthodox Americans themselves. Not only is there already an existing autocephalous Orthodox Church here, but the churches and jurisdictions which still depend upon "Mother Churches" abroad are not, in the most part, made up of recent refugees, or people hoping to return home beyond the ocean. They are not living in a "diaspora," or dispersion "away from home." Their churches have much more stability and permanence than those of the Patriarchates of Alexandria—or even Constantinople. Their missionary outreach is growing. It is time that they make their own voice heard. Orthodox unity in America largely depends on the Orthodox Americans themselves.

January, 1980

What Kind of "American Church"?

In the ongoing discussion of the present and future of Orthodoxy in America, the two most typical and apparently unreconcilable positions are, on the one hand, the defense of ethnicity and ethnic jurisdictions as the only inevitable and permanent form of Orthodox presence in American society, and, on the other hand, an impatient call for Americanization not only in communities where the English language and American culture have become a matter of course, but also in parishes and groups where foreign ethnicity is strong and becomes even stronger through immigration of new members from abroad.

The Orthodox Church in America itself is caught directly in this debate, for it is being most virulently accused by some of still being too "Russian"—although its head and most of its leadership are American and although it can be called "Romanian," "Bulgarian" or "Albanian" as well, since these and other ethnic groups take full part in its structure and policymaking—and by others, of supposedly suffering ethnic traditions in the name of hybrid "Americanism." Some would like it to become and remain forever an "American" jurisdiction, existing side by side with Greek, Russian or Serbian sister-churches; others suggest that it should understand itself as an autocephaly for Russians only and stop pretending to unify all Orthodox Christians living in this country.

All this is rather silly, although one must recognize that some of these criticisms can find grounds in the attitude of those OCA clergy and laity who sometimes adopt one of the views described above.

So, the debate must be transposed on a different level:

solutions must be sought in the nature of the Church herself.
It is obvious that we are faced today with a widespread dis-
belief—among Orthodox Christians themselves—that the
Church *can* transcend ethnicity, politics and human prejudice;
that it does possess a structure, a mission, a purpose, which is
not identifiable with human interests or causes. This is
precisely why, when one speaks of Orthodox norms and of
canonical unity, one is immediately suspected of utopianism.

It remains, however, that if one truly *believes* (and this
is indeed an issue of faith!) that the Church must be first
of all the Church of Christ in its unity, holiness, catholocity
and apostolicity, all priorities must change. If this is impossible, then the Gospel itself is nothing but a utopia. For
example, in the Church of Christ "Americanization" is not
an end in itself, but only a necessary expression of the
Church's mission to Americans, and, among Americans, there
are strong ethnic groups, including Anglo-Saxons, Aleutians,
Blacks, Russians, Greeks, etc., who all deserve consideration
and respect. But none of these groups have the right to
have a church for themselves or, even less, monopolize the
Church as such, and use it in their own particular interests,
or, worse, in the interest of foreign political goals.

What this means in practice is that the Church must be
One. It should be the Church of God and not of men. But
all peoples and groups should be welcome in it. This is
precisely the meaning of "catholicity." Clearly, the progress
made by the OCA in the past ten years indicates that the
"practice of catholicity" is not unrealistic or utopian. But
one should also remember that this progress was achieved
not only through "Americanization"—which is an organic
and necessary process in many parishes and dioceses—but also
by normally accepting a cultural pluralism of legitimate
Orthodox traditions in the framework of the One Church.
If Orthodox unity is to make further progress in the next
decades, it will undoubtedly be based on the same double
principle: mission to America on the one hand, and, on the
other, acceptance of the built-in pluralism which characterizes
the present state of Orthodoxy in the country.

The Greek-American community alone, because of its

numbers, because of its self-conscious faithfulness to the language in which the New Testament itself and the Orthodox liturgical texts were originally written, will hardly let itself integrate soon into an American Orthodox melting pot. Nevertheless, if only contemporary Greek Orthodoxy became a little more open to the missionary dimensions of the Orthodox witness and provided appropriate guidance to its American branch, the latter should undoubtedly occupy a leading position in a canonically united Orthodox Church in America. Shouldn't we welcome that possibility and thank God when it occurs?

So—at least to this writer—it appears that the arduous task of building up the Church in America should be done with patience, charity and wisdom. Otherwise, the Divine light which shines through human weaknesses will remain hidden under the bushel.

October, 1979

The Russian Church and America

On the occasion of the 60th anniversary of the election of Metropolitan Tikhon, a former Archbishop of America (1898-1907), as Patriarch of Moscow and all Russia—an anniversary which is being celebrated in Russia this year— it seems appropriate to recall once more the contributions of the Church of Russia to the establishment and progress of Orthodoxy in America.

From the time of the original mission of the Russian monks to Alaska (1794), the Church of Russia has understood its role in the New World as a mission to Americans, natives or immigrants. Its leadership may have made mistakes and may often have acted inconsistently with its stated intentions, but it has never renounced the mission itself. The goal of its activity was to create an American, not a Russian, Church in America. And it considered this mission not as a betrayal of a "Russian heritage," but as a Christian fulfillment of it.

Archbishop Tikhon himself planned to organize the American Church in such a way that its multiethnic membership and missionary purpose be fully expressed in its structure. The first Orthodox bishop to be consecrated in America was not a Russian, but an Arab, Raphael Hawaweeny, and, in 1905, Tikhon officially proposed to the Holy Synod that the Church in America be recognized as independent (autocephalous).

Since that time Orthodoxy in America has been torn apart with schisms, with the creation of parallel ethnic jurisdictions and with other forms of uncanonical chaos. But again, in 1970, the Russian Church recognized that canonical order and progress could be promoted, not by reaffirming its rights and by claiming power over the American Orthodox, but by giving them freedom to build up their own future. This is the meaning of the status of autocephaly granted to the former "Russian Metropolia," which it fully shares with all those who really desire Orthodox unity, as a united Orthodox Church in America.

Historical facts show that in the past—as in the present—the Russian State has been imperialistic; that it has made attempts at suppressing minorities out of chauvinistic concerns. But it is also a historical fact, especially in the case of America, that the Russian Church, as distinct from the Russian government, has known how to transcend chauvinism and how to be truly "The Church of Christ." Similarly today, the totalitarian and atheistic Soviet regime limits the Church's freedom, controls the statements and actions of the Church's leaders, persecutes those who dare to speak out about the situation, but the Church has succeeded in maintaining the tradition and policies of Patriarch Tikhon concerning America. It has done so not by reaffirming its "rights" and "interests," but by solemnity transferring—through the Tomos of Autocephaly of April 1970—its jurisdictional rights in America to our Autocephalous Church.

It has done so also by recognizing the holiness of St Herman of Alaska and St Innocent, who had proclaimed the need for an English-speaking American church already in 1870. God bless the Russian Church for having remained first Orthodox and only then "Russian."

July, 1977

Why Not Admit It?

This issue of our paper again contains statements by various well-intentioned people referring to the general issue of Orthodox canonical unity in this country. His Eminence, Archbishop Philip of the Antiochian Archdiocese foresees it to happen in twenty-five years. Leon Marinakos of the Hellenic American Congress defends the legitimacy of ethnic cultures and calls for the support of ethnic rights when these are unjustly repressed. On the other hand, Paul David Samir continues the debate on an Orthodox Western rite which had begun in previous issues.

It appears to me that many of the problems which upset the authors—or the readers—of these statements could be solved if the issue of Orthodox unity was properly defined and if one could agree on a proper order of priorities.

First of all, ethnic and cultural pluralism—when it does not degenerate into irrational tribalism—is not supposed to disappear in a united Church. On the contrary, it can enrich it, as it enriches American society. On the other hand, Mr. Marinakos is right to say that ethnicism is not likely to disappear soon—immigrants are still coming in!—so that if one waits until all Orthodox Christians in America become "pure Americans" to make unity a reality, one would have to wait for quite a while. St Paul did not have that kind of patience when he blasted the Corinthians for their divisions. He did not tell them to wait until the time when all Jews would become Greeks, or all Greeks would be Jews. He asked them: "Is Christ divided?" (Please read I Cor 1 in its entirety.)

In the autocephalous Orthodox Church in America today there are many nationalities united in a single canonical structure, sharing responsibility for the election of bishops and gradually discovering the spiritual and practical advantages of unity. Do any of them—Russians, Albanians, Bulgarians, Romanians, Mexicans, Aleuts or "pure Americans"—feel prevented from preserving their cultural identity, or from pursuing legitimate ethnic goals? If they do, let them speak out. Furthermore, it is my firm conviction that a united Orthodox Church would witness much more effectively to the defense of human rights everywhere—including, of course, the beleaguered Greek communities in Istanbul and Cyprus—than separated "ethnic" jurisdictions could ever do, because it would offer better guarantees of fairness and purely Christian concerns. The great authority and influence of the Roman Catholic Church presents a relevant example in this respect.

One can be absolutely sure that canonical unity, assured through the episcopate, would offer a better guarantee for an acceptable cultural pluralism. This point applies equally well to the problem of an Orthodox Western rite—which has been so hotly debated in this paper recently. Clearly, no Orthodox Christian can deny the possibility of liturgical pluralism and the fact that the Christian West possesses treasures of traditions which could enrich our Church today. The issue consists only in defining which of the various Western rites can, in practice, fully express the Orthodox faith and in solving pastoral problems created by isolated Western-rite communities. The courageous initiative taken by the Antiochian Archdiocese in establishing some Western-rite parishes certainly deserves every respect and recognition, but if the same initiative was taken in the name of the whole episcopate of a united Church in America, its significance would have been greater and the pastoral risk smaller, because a united and strong church could, in fact, allow for more internal pluralism and its moves would necessarily be the results of thorough and mature conciliarity.

So, my main point is that unity should be our *first* priority, and it should be promoted primarily here in America. There is strictly no reason to believe that representatives of the various Mother Churches, ill-informed and involved in their own difficulties, will take, on their own, any drastic initiatives at a future council. So far (with the exception of the Church of Russia), they always tended to oppose Orthodox canonical unification in America.

What unity? A unity resulting from gradual reconciliation of little separated factions in each nationality? It is clear that these factions will be the last to accept canonical unity: the reconciliation of such groups as the "Russian Church-in-exile," or the Greek Old Calendarists (more than forty parishes), is much more difficult than an organic and normal unification between major canonical jurisdictions which proclaim that they want unity (see, for example, the editorial "Toward a 'United Orthodox Witness'" in the *Orthodox Observer,* August 16).

One view is that such a unity, if it takes place at all, should result in the OCA abandoning its autocephaly and the other patriarchs—Antioch, Serbia, Romania and Bulgaria—transfering their jurisdiction to Istanbul. A very unlikely eventuality!

So, why not be honest with ourselves and with reality? Why not admit that, if one wants unity, one really wants an Autocephalous Orthodox Church in America? Why not admit that unity in such a church would not mean "submitting" to anyone, but having a common Church, a Church "catholic"? Why not admit that that Church would be in fact of much greater help to the Mother Churches than the present chaos? Why always be looking for substitutes? In any case, as far as we are concerned, we shall never stop asking these questions!

June-July, 1978

II.

DEBATES ON CHURCH ORDER

Conciliarity

"Today the grace of the Holy Spirit gathered us together . . ." These words of an ancient Church hymn, appointed for Palm Sunday, will also be used, according to
tradition, at the opening of the All-American Council at St
Tikhon's on October 20. They express the meaning of the
event: conventions, congresses, assemblies are gathered together by their chairmen or presidents, while a Church council
is gathered together by the Holy Spirit. And it should also
function under the guidance of the same Holy Spirit and not
according to man's will.

Ancient Church councils were primarily assemblies of
bishops, although the other orders of the Church—priests,
deacons, monks, laymen—also occasionally took part. However, the Council of Moscow of 1917-18, which also elected
Patriarch Tikhon, made it a permanent and general rule that
clergy and laity be full voting members of councils. The
Orthodox Church in America inherits this rule from its
Mother Church. It applies it on all levels of Church life: the
parish, the diocese, the entire Church.

It is important that we all realize the remarkable privilege
that we thus enjoy, as well as the tremendous responsibility
which is ours. For, indeed, the conciliar structure of our
Church is a privilege which, unfortunately, is not shared by
many Orthodox today: in Russia, under Communist dictator-
ship, conciliarity has been de facto restricted since the
Council of 1918, and one wonders what kind of council will
be electing the new patriarch next May. Except in Cyprus,
the laity has no voice in the choosing of bishops in the other
Orthodox Churches of the old world. And in America itself,
the head of the Greek Archdiocese is appointed by ecclesias-

tical authorities abroad without consultation with their American flock.

So we are indeed privileged. Let us also be responsible. The Church is not a "democracy" in the human sense. It respects the particular and unique authority of the bishops, without whose sanction no decision can be considered final. But it is not a "monarchy" either, because the bishops' authority is an authority "in" the Church and not "over" the Church.

The Council of October 1970 will have the unique function of serving as a pattern for the future. It must show that the Orthodox Church in America can be a home for all Orthodox Americans and not only for those of Russian extraction. It will be the responsibility of the Council to initiate a revision of our Statute in conformity with the new dimensions of our mission on this continent.

All this can be accomplished only if we are gathered truly by "the grace of the Holy Spirit."

October, 1970

The Eucharist and the Church

One of the most remarkable traits of our life as Orthodox Christians in America during the past decades has been the restoration of the Eucharist, or the Divine Liturgy, as the real spiritual center of our Christian commitment. This occurred with the realization—promoted also in Russia by Fr John of Kronstadt, in Greece by St Nicodemus of the Holy Mountain, and many others—that Holy Communion is offered to all, so that a non-communicating laity practically excludes itself from the Church.

Look now at our All-American Councils: the Divine Liturgy, celebrated every morning with hundreds of communicants, stands as the model which we can use to build the life of our parishes and to make them grow, not as human associations or clubs, or some mysterious holy places where the priests alone and by themselves perform rites watched by the laity, but as revelation of the Kingdom of God for the salvation of all.

But, of course, there are risks and dangers:

— the danger of pietism, if we reduce our participation in the Divine Liturgy to a diffuse feeling of goodness without further responsibility;

— the danger of approaching the Eucharist casually, without regular confession and appropriate preparedness;

— the danger of forgetting that the Son of God, when He became man, did not come to save us—you and me—who happen to know about Him and are members of His Church, but *the whole world*, and that He has entrusted the task of preaching to His disciples, that this task does not consist of words only, but of deeds, thoughts, work, creativity, love for everybody and everything which God created, and a sense of responsibility for those who are in misery—spiritual or material—the "little ones" around us, whom we neglect . . .

The discussion about "Church growth" is about all this; let us learn together how to relate our membership in the Body of Christ, granted to us in the Eucharist, with our task in the world today.

August, 1983

Do We Know the Meaning of the Word "Parish"?

In developing an authentically Christian and Orthodox understanding of our life in the Church, we can sometimes be helped by giving the true meaning to words which are the most obvious and the most usual, but also quite often misunderstood. One of such words is the word "parish," which also exists in other languages under a variety of forms (*parohia, parafia,* etc.). It has been used since the very origins of Christianity to designate a local Christian community. It appears in the writings of the Fathers of the Church and in the canons issued by early councils. The original Greek form in *paroikia,* and it means "temporary," or "secondary" residence.

The permanent "home," the House, is always designated as *oikos.* And for Christians this Home is the Kingdom of God, the Temple where God dwells, the New Jerusalem. However, as long as we are not there yet, God has established for us on earth a temporary home—a tent, where Jesus, the Incarnate Word dwells with us through the Holy Spirit, as He also dwelt with the Hebrews in the desert when they were going towards the Promised Land. However, in the Old Testament this divine presence in a tent had only the symbolic form of an Ark of the Covenant. In the New Testament communion with God is direct and real—in the Body and Blood of Christ.

Thus, the "parish," the *paroikia* gets us very close to Home. But it can serve this purpose only if we see in it not "our" achievement, nor "our" pride, nor—worse still— an ethnic club oriented towards "permanent settlement" in *this* world, away from the Kingdom.

The parish is the place where we offer ourselves to God, where we help others, where we become members of the Church of God, which is called to save, not only us as individuals, as families, as groups, but the whole world, by leading it to the kingdom to come.

Such is the meaning and such are the implications which the Church has placed in this simple and usual word: the Parish. Perhaps we could meditate about it for a while before each parish assembly or parish council we attend.

September, 1981

The Message of Pentecost

According to the Book of Acts, Pentecost is the very birthday of the Church. Different nations heard the message of Christ spoken in their own languages which they could fully understand, and the disciples became so enthused with the new and saving unity received through the Spirit that they "were together and had all things in common"; they "sold their possessions and goods and distributed them to all, as any had need. And day by day, attending the temple together and breaking bread in their homes, they partook of food with glad and generous hearts. . . . And the Lord added to their number day by day those who were being saved" (Acts 2:44-47).

The entire tradition of the Orthodox Church is indeed "pentecostal" in the true sense of the word. The hymns of the day of Pentecost are the best witness to this. One of their major themes is the contrast between the tower of Babel and the descent of the Spirit on Pentecost day. In both events, mankind appears in its linguistic and cultural pluralism, but what a difference in the way this pluralism is understood and used!

In Babel fallen, sinful mankind attempted to build a tower reaching heaven, but in answer to their blasphemous project, God "confused the language of all the earth" (Gen 11:9), so that they ceased to understand each other and their project collapsed. On Pentecost, on the contrary, the various nations heard the same truth and were united into one Church. Their diversity ceased to be an obstacle to unity but was transfigured into becoming the very wealth and variety of divine wisdom. This is best expressed in our *kontakion* for the Feast of Pentecost:

When the Most High came down and confused
the tongues (Gen 11:7), He divided the nations. But
when He distributed the tongues of fire, He called
all to unity. Therefore, with one voice, we glorify
the all-holy Spirit.

Seen in this light, the Feast of Pentecost provides the
clearest pattern for the Church at all times and in all places.
Moreover, here in America, our very belonging to the
Church, established on Pentecost, is put to test. As there, in
Jerusalem, we are challenged by the Spirit to answer the call
to unity. But we clearly do not understand the call and prefer
to live in the categories established in Babel: our ethnic cultures and languages keep us separated. And what is even
more extraordinary, some patriarchs and bishops who claim
to be successors of the Apostles and, therefore, heirs to the
gifts of Pentecost, are making every effort to perpetuate
the division of the Church and to maintain their flocks in
submission to the unredeemed and fallen structures of ethnicity and phyletism.

Let there be no mistake: the issue is clearly one of truth,
or heresy, and the struggle for Orthodox unity in America
is the same as the one which was waged by the Fathers
against the divisions which plagued the Church in the past.
The only difference is that today no one has yet dared to
change the teachings of the Church formally: everyone still
sings the *kontakion* of Pentecost, albeit in a language which
the faithful do not understand. So the problem for us Orthodox is to become what we already claim to be; to strive for
consistency to realize the incredible hiatus which exists between our principles and reality, and to try to overcome
it. Yes, since Pentecost, the Holy Spirit abides in the Church.
But do we want to be the Church, or do we prefer the
catastrophe of Babel?

June, 1979

Towards a Great Orthodox Council?

Several pan-Orthodox meetings representing the various autocephalous Churches have met periodically since 1961 in order to prepare a forthcoming council of the whole Orthodox Church. Out of humility (or caution), the term "ccumenical council" is being avoided in the preliminary documents, but in the minds of the drafters the idea that, if held, the council may act as an ecumenical council is not excluded.

Normally, there would be very reason to rejoice that these preparations are taking place: world Orthodoxy needs unity, the world needs the voice of Orthodoxy; the tremendous crisis of Western Christianity places on Orthodoxy an exceptional responsibility and, more explicitly than ever, calls it to become a witness of Christ's truth in its fullness. It is also obvious that the faithful need guidance in disciplinary matters. An end should be put to the chaotic squabbles which compromise the Orthodox Church in the eyes of the world.

Several youth meetings, among them the Assembly of Orthodox French-speaking youth in Annecy (France), have expressed great hopes concerning the council. In fact, they look at it as the providential event which will solve the problems of Orthodoxy today. At the same time, a highly respected voice—that of the elderly and venerable Serbian Archimandrite Justin Popovich—warns against the very idea of a council under the present circumstances: most Orthodox Churches are in Communist-dominated countries and are, therefore, deprived of freedom of speech. He also implies that the agenda of the future council, as it was prepared under the leadership of the Ecumenical Patriarchate of Istanbul, has not been worked out sufficiently and is labeled in a way that does not correspond to the Tradition of the

Fathers. Under those circumstances a council can only be futile and even dangerous.

With some qualifications, this writer shares the point of view of the respected Serbian theologian. On the purely practical level, one fails to see how the Soviet government, and the governments of its satellite countries, would presently allow the entire Orthodox episcopate of those countries to go abroad. It is equally difficult to conceive that a true "Great Council" could meet in a Communist country, where no Church assembly thus far was allowed any really free deliberation. The survival of the Orthodox Church in those countries, based upon the simple and stubborn faith of millions, is a miracle in itself, but it is being bought at a very high price of hierarchical silence and of external submission to the will of the State.

It is actually refreshing that several representatives of the Patriarchate of Moscow have privately expressed doubts about the possibility of a council. I presonally would be very suspicious of a great enthusiasm on their part on this question. How easy it would have been for them to wreck, compromise and ruin Orthodox conciliarity, if a council were held in which they would have the massive representation to which they are entitled! This would undoubtedly be their goal, if they were only "Communists in disguise," as some would like to see them! But apparently they are unwilling to assume that role.

Another major obstacle to the calling of a council in the near future is the present state of its preparation. It seems that its organizers—mainly representatives of the Ecumenical Patriarchate—have tried their best to avoid real issues and to concentrate on peripherals, such as the discipline of fasting, the publication of a "scientific" text of Scripture and generalities on the "codification of canons," or abstractions like the "source of revelation." Fortunately, at the last meeting of the pan-Orthodox commission in Chambesy (Switzerland, July 1971), it was demanded that the agenda of the prospective council be modified. It is symptomatic, however, that such a burning question as the canonical structure of the "diaspora" was at no time even officially mentioned during the work of preparation, although the issue is on the agenda as it stands now.

Do we have, then, to be wholly pessimistic about the future of Orthodox "conciliarity"—the famed "sobornost"—on the world level? I do not think so. And I certainly do not want to pour cold water on the enthusiastic expectations of so many Orthodox Christians. But I believe that real results could be achieved only if we became more humble, more practical, more Christian also, and less engulfed in Byzantine politics, coupled with mythomania, which often characterizes our public relations and also, unfortunately, our relations among ourselves.

Certainly, the various pan-Orthodox commissions must continue their work. They have achieved significant results in limited areas, such, for example, as our dialogue with the "Non-Chalcedonian" Eastern Churches. But they must also begin to tackle the real basic problems of the Orthodox Church today. There is much talk, for example, about the conflict between Constantinople and Moscow on the problem of the autocephaly of the Orthodox Church in America. Why is it that no commission—official or non-official—representing all the Orthodox Churches ever got to discuss it for over two years? It is obvious that a solution to this problem is a pre-condition of a fruitful conciliar work. Similarly, pan-Orthodox commissions could give valuable direction to our activities in the various ecumenical agencies, if only they got into the concrete problems, instead of limiting themselves to generalities and platitudes. No one would challenge the "primacy" of Constantinople in initiating such consultations.

These should be the limited and immediate goals of our "conciliarity." These goals are achievable. I do not deny that God could also perform a miracle and gather a General Council which would be fully independent of the Soviets, the Turks, the Greek colonels, and transcend all our limitations. I do believe in miracles, but I also know that we should not tempt God by counting too much on miracles for which we may not be ready.

February, 1972

New Moves Towards a Pan-Orthodox Council

After several years of practical silence on the issue, the Ecumenical Patriarchate of Constantinople has taken new steps towards calling a council of all the Orthodox Churches. Led by Metropolitan Meliton of Chelcedon—who was granted an exit-visa by the Turkish authorities on the occasion of his attendance at the Assembly of the World Council of Churches in Nairobi—a delegation of the patriarchate visited most Orthodox centers in Europe (including Moscow) and came up with the plan of a consultation to be held this fall in Switzerland.

Agendas for a prospective council were already examined at several pan-Orthodox encounters in the sixties. They included ambitious theological schemes and seemed rather unrealistic to many. This time the agenda proposed by the Ecumenical Patriarchate is very concrete. It responds to urgent needs of contemporary Orthodoxy. It is urgent, for example, to start a frank discussion of the role and responsibilities of the Ecumenical Patriarchate in the concert of Orthodox Churches; it is even more urgent to face the scandal of jurisdictional divisions in Western Europe, in Australia and particularly in America. The very important issues raised between Orthodox authorities in 1970 on the occasion of the establishment of the autocephalous church in America did not lead so far to official consultations on a pan-Orthodox level. They are now officially on the agenda of the forthcoming consultation.

So far, it appears that the Orthodox Church in America has not been invited to take official part in that meeting. Officially recognized by the patrirchates of Moscow, Georgia and Bulgaria, and the autocephalous Churches of Poland and Czechoslovakia, it still awaits the official recognition of the other local Churches, altheough *de facto* it does entertain sacramental and brotherly relations with all of them. At an initial stage of the debate they may want to discuss their attitude among themselves. It remains, however, that no real solution can be found unless all the parties involved, including our Church, engage in brotherly consultation. One would hope that ways can be found to secure such consultation without further delay.

The establishment of a stable and canonically permanent American Orthodoxy is a momentous and irreversible fact, one of the few really positive events of Orthodox history in the twentieth century. One cannot ignore it without being unfaithful to the catholic truth of Orthodoxy. And—as we have repeatedly indicated in our editorials—American autocephaly is perfectly compatible with ethnic tradition and with the traditional role of ancient patriarchates. But the proper balance of all the various elements of the problem can be found only through mutual respect and conciliarity. We pray that the present round of "preconciliar" activity will bring about the desired unity.

One last remark: In our personal opinion the other points of the proposed agenda—date of Easter, changes in the marriage discipline for clergy—should, at present, be simply dropped from the list. They can only divide the Orthodox once more, and, in any case, they involve decrees of the ancient Councils which cannot be tampered with easily. Moreover, it does not seem to us that the drafters of the agenda gave sufficient thought to the issue of "second marriage" of priests: Scripture itself affirms that bishops and priests are "husbands of one wife" (1 Tim 3:2; Tit 1:6). Absolute monogamy is an *ideal* for all Christians, but a *formal requirement* for clergy. No council is empowered to change the doctrine revealed in the New Testament.

September, 1976

The Council: Where and When?

The major objection raised by some Orthodox Churches—primarily by the Ecumenical Patriarchate of Constantinople—against the establishment of the autocephalous Orthodox Church in America on April 10, 1970, was that this was a "unilateral act" of the Church of Russia which, to be fully legitimate, needed the endorsement of a Great Council of the entire Orthodox Church.

We will not discuss here once more the issue whether this objection was valid or not. But it is obvious that wherever and whenever there is disagreement, the tradition of the Church recommends that a conciliar procedure take place. Since there is disagreement in this particular case, all Orthodox Christians should hope that a council can resolve it. In any case, the *Tomos* of Autocephaly itself presupposes that full Orthodox unity in this country cannot be enforced unilaterally by any Church, and that an agreement between all Orthodox Churches is a prerequisite of unity. So there is a basic agreement that a council would be the normal procedure to follow.

In the years following 1970, the Patriarchate of Constantinople has repeatedly announced that a council was forthcoming. Preparatory meetings were held. The issue of Orthodox canonical unity in Western countries was placed on the agenda. The various Orthodox Churches were consulted and gave their opinions on the subject.

But, more than nine years have passed. There is no evidence that either a date or a place for the future Council have been selected. Meanwhile, unilateral actions continue. For example, the Patriarchate of Constantinople has approved the new Charter of the Greek Archdiocese which establishes, in an official way, the totally uncanonical coexistence of several Orthodox bishops in the same city. Other Orthodox patriarchates—for example, the Patriarchate of Romania—seem to endorse the ethnic principle as the only normal criterion of Church structure in America. So, there is no council, no consultation, no public debate, but there is implicit agreement that division and "phyletism" are inevitable.

This situation is deplorable, and it cannot continue. The various Orthodox patriarchates in the Middle East and in Communist countries may well be paralyzed and unable to take action, but they have neither the right nor the ultimate power to paralyze the progress of Orthodoxy in America. So, it is time for all the Orthodox in America—not only in the OCA, but also in the jurisdictions which still depend upon Mother Churches abroad—to demand an end to double-talk. A true Orthodox Great Council, if it is properly convoked and is truly representative of the entire Church, would undoubtedly endorse the only possible canonical solution for America: a united and autocephalous Church.

We call for such a council and we pray that the existing obstacles to its meeting may soon be removed. We also believe that most of those who object against the already-existing autocephaly of the OCA know very well that the future council will have really no other alternative to offer.

In any case, it is neither realistic nor ethical to mislead the media with announcements of a forthcoming council, when one does not really believe that it can be held. It is better to attempt a step by step approach and build upon the canonical foundation, which has been laid in 1970. When the Apostles were establishing the Church after the Resurrection of Jesus, they were not appealing to forthcoming councils to solve their problemse: they met, they consulted, they invoked the Holy Spirit and they acted!

July, 1979

A Welcome Public Debate

The recent events in the life of the Orthodox Church in Finland have provoked a public debate which is summarized in the remarkably frank, honest and open article by His Eminence, Archbishop Paul of Carelia and all Finland. Unfortunately, it is rather rare that Orthodox primates and bishops follow the example of the ancient holy fathers of the Church and speak openly and freely about the contemporary problems of the Church. It is more usual for them to practice confidential diplomacy. Of course, one can sympathize with those of them, who find themselves under the direct pressure of their governments and are not free to speak. But it remains true that the problems facing the Orthodox Church in the contemporary world cannot be solved without free debate. If such a debate does not take place, there is no hope whatsoever that the preparations for a Pan-Orthodox Council, initiated by the Patriarchate of Constantinople, will ever lead to positive results.

In his article Archbishop Paul discusses primarily the case of the Church of Finland which has the fully justified desire—in spite of its small size—to become an autocephalous Church and cease to be an administrative dependency of a foreign patriarchate, which is itself tied up by Turks. But he also unveils the present state of the pan-Orthodox debate on autocephaly—a debate which cannot remain confidential anymore. Opinions different from that of Constantinople have been expressed not only by the Church of Russia, but also by the Churches of Antioch and Romania.

It is clear that, in the coming months, the case of Finland will serve as a test—a rather easy test, in fact, where the Ecumenical Patriarchate has not as yet lost all its cards. By

128

a show of understanding, it can still grant Finland its auto-cephaly and make everyone happy. But one must also hope that the precedent will serve America, as well—a much more difficult situation, where solutions are urgently needed. The present—inevitably public—debate clearly shows the real issues: Are the various Orthodox patriarchates abroad ready to transcend their particular, nationalistic and political goals and commit themselves to the interests of "catholic" Ortho-doxy of the Church itself? Do the Orthodox themselves, who presently live in America, whatever their ethnic background, want to be the Church and not simply use facilities and structures of the Church to promote particular cultural or political concerns?

Experience seems to indicate that the answer to the first question must unfortunately remain negative. To me per-sonally, the only hope for the future is that the autocephalous Orthodox Church in America answers with a resolute "yes" to the second question.

April, 1979

Orthodoxy Needs a Center

The recent death of Ecumenical Patriarch Athenagoras I and the election of his successor raises again the long-standing problem of the exact role and function of the Ecumenical Patriarchate in the Orthodox world.

As is well known, the canons of the second and fourth Ecumenical Councils assign to the Bishop of Constantinople the second place in the "hierarchy of honor" of the major episcopal sees of the Church. The first place, at that time, belonged to the Bishop of Rome. The same canons clearly specify the reason why this eminent position is assigned to the Bishop of Constantinople. The reason is sociopolitical: Constantinople—also called "New Rome"—was "the seat of the emperor and the Senate" (canon 28 of the Council of Chalcedon). Obviously, at the time when there was an empire—which was theoretically universal and Christian—it appeared natural, and even necessary, that the political and ecclesiastical centers of the Christian world would be located in the same place.

After the schism with Rome, Constantinople was recognized as "first among equals" by the other Orthodox patriarchs. However, the very reasons why the Orthodox Church rejected the primacy of the pope, categorically excluded any possibility of recognizing and assigning a similar "papal" position to Constantinople. "The Ecumenical Patriarch" in the Orthodox world could enjoy a certain priority in common affairs, but could never become the "head" of the entire Church. Christ alone was such a head.

However, as long as the empire existed, the Ecumenical Patriarch enjoyed, in fact, a great power. The missionary and administrative activity of the "Great Church" of Constantinople nourished for centuries the Slavic Churches. Its historic achievements are truly remarkable. So that even after the fall of Constantinople to the Turks (1453), the Orthodox Churches continued to respect the tradition of Constantinople's moral primacy, even if the reasons which motivated its elevation had disappeared. In fact, Turkish control over the patriarchate greatly reduced its prestige outside of Turkish-contrtolled territory. The great Russian Church, for example, was never under Turkish rule. The Churches of the Balkans, as they achieved independence from the Turks, liberated themselves also from the ecclesiastical control of Constantinople. In spite of the fact that throughout the Turkish period the Ecumenical Patriarchate has always been the center of Greek nationalism, independent Greece was the first Balkan country to reject Constantinople's jurisdiction and to become autocephalous (1833).

Gradually, the situation of the Ecumenical Patriarchate became more and more pathetic. The remarkable efforts of Athenagoras I to build up the prestige of the patriarchate, and even to make it appear as a sort of Eastern papacy, had some effect upon American journalists—who speak of him and of his successor in truly papist terms—but not on the Turkish government, whose intention is clearly to reduce the patrirchate to the spiritual leadership of 20,000 Orthodox Turkish citizens and to suppress it as an international center. Actually, even under Athenagoras, no international meeting could be held in Istanbul (the present name of Constantinople), and, of course, the entire staff of the patriarchate had to be made up of Greeks from Turkey.

These are the facts of the situation, and there is little that anybody—even the Greek government, interested politically in Constantinople's prestige—can do about it.

It remains, however, that Orthodoxy needs a center. There was never a time in the entire history of our Church when universal Orthodoxy did not recognize a center of unity, of common action, of common witness. At the very beginning, as described in the Acts of the Apostles, the center was in Jerusalem. Later, by common consent, Rome was seen as a center of unity. Finally, as we have shown above, this center was located in Constantinople.

It is clear that in the present—apparently irreversible political situation—there is no possibility to restore in Istanbul an international center able to exercise a meaningful leadership. Fortunately, the Orthodox conception of the Church excludes that any city, any place, would possess this characteristic and exclusive privilege: our entire polemics against Rome were based on this point. It remains, also, that the Orthodox Church is a conservative and traditional Church, and it is quite concerned with continuity and tradition. Finally, it is desirable that the center of world Orthodoxy would not be under the exclusive influence of a big political power or of a particular ethnic group. A transfer of the "center" to Moscow, for example, is presently unthinkable.

All these aspects of the question being taken into consideration, we see no possibility for the future except in the project—already proposed by the Romanian Church forty years ago—that the center be located on the ecclesiastical territory of the ecumenical patriarchate, but not in Turkey— for example, on Mount Athos or on the island of Rhodes— and that the staff of the patriarchate become sufficiently international to represent all the Orthodox Churches.

At the time when this editorial is being written, it is not yet known how the various Orthodox patriarchates and churches will react to the events, and even whether they will unanimously recognize Demetrios I, whose election took place under such obvious Turkish pressure, but we can be sure that if he courageously proposes the reform described above, the Ecumenical Patriarchate will regain its prestige and become really a working center of Orthodoxy.

August-September, 1972

NEEDED: The Ecumenical Patriarchate

The protests recently voiced by Archbishop Iakovos and supported by the Roman Catholic leadership on behalf of the Patriarchate of Constantinople and the Greek community in Istanbul, and the rebuke which these protests received from Metropolitan Meliton, illustrate the tragic position of the patriarchate in Turkey. Just as the leadership of the Russian Church denies the existence of religious persecution in Russia, so Metropolitan Meliton voices his confidence in the good relationships between Greeks and Turks in Istanbul and rejects intervention by "foreigners." In the two cases the stakes are not the same in terms of numbers—fifty million faithful in the Soviet Union, a remnant of 6,000 Greeks in Istanbul—but the methods, the attitudes and the lack of freedom are basically identical.

However, in the case of Constantinople, there is another dimension to the problem: its patriarchate, for the past many centuries, has been recognized as having a certain responsibility for the entire Church as a center of consensus with a "primacy of honor." This is why it is called the "Ecumenical Patriarchate." Misinformed journalists sometimes identify the Ecumenical Patriarch's position to that of the pope in Roman Catholicism, which is, of course, quite absurd, but it is unquestionable that the Orthodox conception of the Church recognizes the need for a leadership of the world episcopate, for a certain spokesmanship by the first patriarch, for a ministry of coordination without which conciliarity is impossible. Because Constantinople, also called "New Rome," was the capital of the Empire, the ecumenical council designated its bishop—in accordance with the practical realities of that day—for this position of leader-

ship, which he has kept until this day, even if the Empire
does not exist anymore. The Patriarchate of Constantinople
certainly cannot claim infallibility—for so many of its in-
cumbents throughout its long history were condemned for
various heresies: Nestorianism, Monotheletism, Iconoclasm,
Uniatism and even Protestantism (in the case of Cyril
Lukaris)—but it was never deprived of its "ecumenicity,"
being always answerable to the conciliar consciousness of the
Church.

In the present chaotic years, the Orthodox Church could
indeed use wise, objective and authoritative leadership of the
Ecumenical Patriarchate. Would it not be his obligation, for
example, to come up with a positive, constructive and practical
solution to the jurisdictional pluralism in America?

The essential dimension of the situation seems to be
completely lost in the various actions which aim at simply
"saving" and "maintaining" the patriarchate's present position in Istanbul. For it is quite clear that the present restric-
tions placed on it by the Turks are preventing the patriarchate
from fulfilling its role meaningfully. It appears, therefore,
that protests and pressures are not to be directed towards
the simple maintenance of the present *status quo* which, if
it continues, would ruin the prestige of the patriarchate
completely and would create conditions under which the
possibility of setting up another center will be raised in a
formal way at the forthcoming Pan-Orthodox Council (a
possibility which is not excluded by the canons, since the
Orthodox Church recognizes that the center moved from
Rome to Constantinople).

The protests and pressures should therefore be directed
towards one of the two following alternatives:

1.   The patriarchate, in its traditional residence, is formally recognized by Turkey as having an international role,
is provided with proper facilities, is allowed not only to
receive visitors, but also to set up an instructional staff—
for, indeed, if the patrirchate is "ecumenical," it needs the
permanent advice and cooperation of representatives from
all Orthodox Churches—and to be allowed to use as its
cathedral St Sophia or at least one of the other major

Christian shrines of the city, now transformed into mosques or museums. There would be a clear political gain for Turkey in the eyes of world opinion if it allowed this.

2. If this first—and clearly preferable—alternative proves impractical, the patriarchate should be moved to a location where the above conditions for normal functioning can be met.

All Orthodox Christians—and indeed all men and women of decency—should sympathize not only with the human tragedy of the Greeks in Istanbul, but also with the emotional and cultural attachment which all Greeks—and certainly all the Orthodox—feel for the city of Constantine. To abandon that city forever is indeed an agony! But the Orthodox Church needs an Ecumenical Patriarchate and cannot allow it simply to wither away together with the Greek colony in Istanbul.

One hears, from time to time, the argument that a patriarchate removed from Constantinople could not be recognized as "ecumenical" anymore and that it would be challenged by Moscow. This argument is without any foundation, as historical precedents clearly show: the patriarchate has been in exile already once (in Nicea, 1204-1261); the present Patriarchate of Antioch is not located in Antioch but in Damascus, Syria, etc. Moreover, the Patriarchate of Moscow has let it be known that it would not challenge the primacy of Constantinople (and who would support Moscow in such a challenge?), if it is removed to a location within the limits of its traditional territory, e.g., the Greek islands or northern Greece. A problem would arise only with a relocation in non-traditional places such as Switzerland or New York. . . .

So, one wonders whether one does not do a disservice to the Ecumenical Patriarchate and to universal Orthodoxy by simply trying to maintain an unattainable *status quo* instead of *facing the above alternatives squarely.*

April, 1978

Orthodox Churches Meet in Switzerland

Since 1961, several official inter-Orthodox meetings were convened upon the initiative of the Ecumenical Patriarchate of Constantinople in order to prepare an agenda for a forthcoming "great" or "ecumenical" council of the Orthodox Church. The meetings had the very fortunate effect of promoting the spirit of Orthodox unity and of dispelling the impression that the various Orthodox Churches are nothing but separate ethnic groups and do not constitute one universal Church. However, the tentative agenda worked out at these meetings gave the rather strange impression that the participants themselves were not quite sure why a council was necessary. In the past all councils of the Church were convened in order to face a concrete and obvious issue, generally a heresy which needed to be condemned or a doctrinal issue which needed solution. The pan-Orthodox meetings of the sixties included in the tentative agenda a collection of abstract themes, such as the composition of an Orthodox "Confession of Faith," and the preparation of a common critical text of Scripture. There was actually neither the need nor the possibility for a council to deal with such matters.

Meanwhile, the Orthodox Church was indeed facing a crisis and confronted with heresy. The crisis consisted in the ever-increasing canonical chaos which prevailed in areas where no traditional and unified Orthodox canonical structure was in existence (America, Western Europe, Australia). The heresy—which was already labeled as "phyletism" by the Council of Constantinople of 1872—was that ethnic allegiance replaced the holy canons and the most basic principles of the Orthodox doctrine of the Church in shaping the organization of Orthodoxy in the *diaspora*: the "Greek

Church," the "Russian Church," the "Serbian Church" and many others existed in parallel organizations on the same territory. "Phyletism" (from the Greek *phyle*—"nation" or "race") was making Orthodox missionary witness impossible; it identified the Orthodox Catholic faith with ethnic folklore in the eyes of those who did not belong to Eastern European ethnic minorities; it made political feuds and divisions inside each group practically inevitable.

In 1965 the Standing Conference of Orthodox Bishops tried to place the issue on the agenda of a pan-Orthodox meeting in Geneva but was rebuked by the Patriarchate of Constantinople.

Since then the situation has changed radically. By far the major element in the change has been the decision taken by the Patriarchate of Moscow in 1970 to establish in America an independent, autocephalous Church whose doors would be opened to Orthodox Christians of all backgrounds and whose exclusive mission would be to Americans. Since the establishment of the autocephaly, the OCA—uniting in its fold Albanians, Romanians, Mexicans, Eskimos, Aleutians, Indians, as well as Russians and Slavs of all origins, and making an ever-increasing appeal to Americans of all backgrounds—has known only progress, in spite of criticisms and fears expressed in the name of "ethnicism."

The inter-Orthodox meeting held at the Center of the Ecumenical Patriarchate in Chambesy, near Geneva, on November 21-30, approved a tentative agenda which lists the issues of the Orthodox *diaspora* and the procedure for the establishment of new autocephalous and autonomous churches as top priority. This is tremendous progress indeed. One should also welcome the elimination from the agenda of the issue of second marriage of priests which was suggested (in our opinion quite thoughtlessly) by some representatives of Constantinople.

The Orthodox Church in America (OCA), which is officially recognized by six local Churches while others withhold judgment, was not represented at the Chambesy meeting. However regrettable its temporary absence may be, one can understand that the "older Churches" must first make up their minds on the disagreement which exists among them about the procedure for establishing new autocephalous churches. The disagreement does not concern only the OCA; there is no agreement either concerning the Churches of Georgia, Czechoslovakia, Poland and Japan.

One should hope that at least some of these differences can be solved before the next meeting of the preparatory conference which is scheduled, in principle, for next year. The solution requires, on behalf of some leaders of "older" Churches, a much greater awareness of the real situation in the *diaspora,* and particularly in America. This awareness unfortunately does not seem to exist and a purely "colonial" spirit dominates some minds. If it persists, no solution can obviously be reached. The Orthodox Church in America will certainly be ready to contribute in every possible way to the preliminary process. But no decision can obviously be taken without a fully representative council of *all* the Churches, including the Orthodox Church in America. In any case, our Primate, His Beatitude, Metropolitan Ireney, has been informed that the patriarchates and autocephalous Churches which do recognize the autocephaly of the Orthodox Church in America will not participate in a council, unless it is fully representative.

Whatever the difficulties and the imperfections marking this new round of pan-Orthodox consultations, the leadership provided by the Ecumenical Patriarchate can be commended for its initiative and for its courage. This time it does not shy away from the real issues. The "primacy of honor" which it exercises among the various Orthodox Churches will undoubtedly be enhanced if, as a result of the Chambesy meeting, a consensus emerges, leading to canonical order and united witness of the Orthodox Church in the Western world.

January, 1977

Church or–"Diaspora"?

Since the settlement of many Orthodox Christians in America, Western Europe and other parts of the world—a major twentieth-century development in the history of Christianity—it became customary to speak of an Orthodox "diaspora" outside the borders of the so-called "Orthodox countries." Not many people, however, have spent much time reflecting on the meaning of that term, and on the implications of its use in debates about "canonicity," "mission" and other basic concepts of Church life.

The term "diaspora," translated as "dispersion," designates a well-known biblical concept (see John 7:35; James 1:1; 1 Peter 1:1): the Jews, who were obliged to leave the land of Israel and to live among the "gentiles." For them, exile was necessarily a calamity, since all Jews were bound by the very meaning of their faith to hope for a return to the "promised land." Their sojourn "among the gentiles" was a consequence of political catastrophies, often interpreted as God's punishment. Even if, in individual cases, this going-abroad was provoked by personal or economic reasons, and represented a free decision, it was still an essentially *temporary* solution: the Jew, his family and his descendants still belonged to "Sion" spiritually.

Now, for Christians, there is no more "Sion" on earth: they long for a "New Jerusalem" in the Kingdom of God. In a sense, therefore, *all* Christians are in "diaspora," or in "dispersion," but not because they were expelled from their country, but because "they have no continuing city" here, but "seek one to come" (Heb 13:14).

The Church is always called to manifest and anticipate this Kingdom, the true homeland of Christians. The Divine

Liturgy starts with this proclamation: "Blessed is the Kingdom of ths Father, and of the Son, and of the Holy Spirit."
The Kingdom, the true "homeland," is *wherever* the Liturgy
is celebrated, but it is not limited geographically; it is not
tied up to any country or city on earth. Therefore, if we speak
of the contemporary Orthodox "diaspora," we do not speak
on spiritual, biblical terms, but in empirical and secular
categories. And if we let the Church be tied up with these
categories, *we betray the Kingdom of God itself.*

The above observations are of great importance for the
future of the Orthodox Church in America and in other
lands. Much debate goes on, for example, about the canonical
status of the "diaspora": the Ecumenical Patriarchate of
Constantinople formally claims rights of jurisdiction over
the entire Orthodox "diaspora," while exercising it in fact
only in the case of the Greeks—and some other ethnic
groups—but without the consent of their own "Mother
Churches." Most "Mother Churches" want to govern their
own "diasporas" themselves, disregarding Constantinople's
claim completely, basing their canonical thinking on purely
ethnic considerations. As a result, the *de facto* organization
of the Orthodox Church—in America, in Europe and elsewhere—follows completely empirical and secular categories,
which lead to canonical chaos and reflects a real spiritual
and theological crisis.

The question of the "diaspora" is on the agenda of the
future Pan-Orthodox Council. Reference to this council is
often made to justify inaction and passivity; but is there any
serious assurance that it is going to meet soon? And if so,
what kind of preparation is being made to obtain a real discussion of the extremely touchy and politically-loaded issue
of the "diaspora"? To my knowledge, none of the Pan-
Orthodox meetings ever dared to face the issue directly,
the participants being afraid of serious disagreements and
conflicts. But is it seriously possible to expect the future
council—if it ever meets—to take any decision without
preliminary groundwork?

The establishment of the autocephalous Orthodox Church
in America in 1970 was the first real step in the direction

of a solution. This step was taken on the assumption that the Church cannot—and should not—be organized in America in terms of a "diaspora," as if Orthodox Americans were all longing to "return home" to Europe. The Orthodox Church of Russia was able to take this step simply because it *never* thought of its work in America in terms of "diaspora," but established it, first in Alaska (1799), then in the States (1870), as a "mission." And any mission must lead to the establishment of a permanent organized Church. Obviously, it would have been better if the decision could have been taken by common consent, and if it was supported by the Ecumenical Patriarchate which, by common Orthodox consent, does possess a leadership responsibility (but no infallibility) in Orthodoxy. But ultimately it is quite immaterial who did the right thing. The establishment of the Orthodox Church in America, its increasing self-assurance and stability, its steady growth during the past three years, are all signs that a genuine Orthodoxy in America is here to stay, whatver efforts are being made—on wrong spiritual and canonical assumptions—to reduce it to a "diaspora" status.

March, 1974

What Is the "Diaspora"?

The Greek term *diaspora* is frequently used to designate Orthodox communities established in various countries of the Western world. Churchmen and canonists of the Mother Churches of Eastern Europe are debating their respective rights. The Ecumenical Patriarchate sometimes claims (on the basis of a mention in canon 28 of the Council of Chalcedon that it is allowed to appoint bishops in "barbarian lands") the exclusive right to administer the *diaspora*. Most other Churches, however, maintain their own *"diasporas"* under their own control on the basis of ethnic allegiance. This situation has created everywhere—and particularly in America—a canonical disorder from which the Orthodox witness to the contemporary world suffers greatly.

In order to contribute meaningfully to a truly Orthodox and Christian solution of the problem—which is point 1 on the agenda of pan-Orthodox meetings—the very concept of *"diaspora"* needs clarification. It is our contention that its indiscriminate use obscures the issues and prevents a solution.

The Greek word *diaspora* is a biblical term and has a perfectly adequate English equivalent: "dispersion." It designates the Jews who live outside of Israel, but—as it is proper to all true adherents of Judaism—consider Israel as "promised land," nourish the hope of returning there some day and maintain strong cultural and political loyalty to its interests. The Jewish attachment to the land of Israel is based on the very nature of Old Testament religion: it is sanctioned by the promises of God Himself.

Can this concept be transferred to the religion of the New Testament? Clearly not. In the Lord Jesus Christians discover the ultimate reason why Israel had been originally

142

chosen: the Messiah—i.e., Jesus Himself—was to appear there "from the seed of David." However, His appearance and His teaching bring salvation to all nations. Neither Israel, nor any other country, can make an exclusive claim to divine election anymore. Israel was indeed elected, but the goal of that election has now been reached: the God of Israel has been revealed in Jesus as Lord and Savior of the whole world.

But since there is no "promised land" any longer (except the heavenly Jerusalem, Apoc 21-22), there cannot be any *"diaspora,"* or "dispersion," either. Or else Christians can all be seen as being in "dispersion"—whether they live in the East or in the West, whether they form a majority or a minority in a given country's population—until they find their true home in God's heavenly kingdom. This is why the very term *"diaspora"* or "dispersion" is never used in the canons of the Orthodox Church

It is only on the basis of these unquestionable facts of the Christian faith that problems of contemporary Orthodoxy should be resolved.

There are indeed millions of Orthodox Christians living in the West whose religious destiny is not to seek and to maintain allegiance to some distant "promised lands," but to be the Church of God in countries where God's providence has brought them. One should also emphasize a fact which the leadership of "Mother Churches" so often ignores: in America, with the Alaskan mission being almost two centuries old, with an ever-increasing number of native Americans finding their spiritual home in Orthodoxy, with the East European background of many being a thing of the past, there exists already an Orthodox Church which is as "American" as other churches can be called "Russian" or "Greek."

We have emphasized many times in the past that Orthodox unity does not presuppose the forced Americanization of anyone, that cultural and linguistic pluralism is a sign of the Church's catholicity and is, therefore, fully legitimate, that Orthodox unity will come by mutual consent, not by a triumph of one group over another. But it will come only when we will stop defining our "dispersion" as a "dispersion" from earthly motherlands (however precious and legitimate our foreign cultural ties may remain), and recognize that the Church of God transcends all ethnic allegiances and should be organized as the "one," as the "holy," as the "catholic," and as the "apostolic" Church wherever it finds itself.

The remarkable and consoling fact of the present situation in the Orthodox world is that the above principle is admitted as normative by the major parties concerned, including the Patriarchates of Constantinople and Moscow (see their correspondence on the occasion of the American autocephaly, 1970). It remains to put the principles into practice.

February, 1977

Syndesmos, a Hope for Orthodoxy

In our divided world, the Orthodox Church sometimes appears as helpless in overcoming the factionalism, the divisiveness, the ethnic defensiveness which keep its various communities apart from each other. There exists, however, one truly pan-Orthodox organization which, for over thirty years, has succeeded in serving and realizing the universal calling of the Orthodox message.

This organization is "Syndesmos." The name is the Greek term for "bond" and is inspired by the words of St Paul: "Above all these things put on love, which is the *bond* of perfection" (Col 4:14). Its goals are modest and clearly defined: to serve as a catalyst for joint action and unity between Orthodox youth organizations, or agencies responsible for youth work, or simply youth groups. The activities of "Syndesmos" do not pretend to involve the hierarchy of the Church, but the statutes require that member-organizations be in good standing with their respective ecclesiastical authorities.

The membership is extremely varied. In some countries, there exist numerous and active youth movements. In others, such movements would be illegal. As a result, "Syndesmos" accepts within its fold such groups as the student bodies of individual theological schools.

Every three years a general assembly is held. Last summer it met in Crete, Greece. The preceding one had been convened in New Valaamo, Finland, where the General Secretariat is located. The last assembly elected Mark Stokoe, an American and a graduate of St Vladimir's Seminary, as General Secretary and made the decision to hold the next general assembly in the United States in 1986*

*The 1986 Assembly was actually held in England. *Ed.*

One of the points on the agenda of the last meeting of the North American member-groups, held on January 14, 1984, was to begin the preparation of that event.

"Syndesmos" deserves the support of all. Having received the blessings not only from the Ecumenical Patriarchate, but also from all the other churches with which it is in touch, it has promoted the ideal of Orthodox unity and encouraged the free discussion of all the problems of contemporary Orthodoxy. It has inspired generations of Orthodox young people in their dedication to the Church. It has initiated Orthodox missionary activity. Here, in North America, it can help us to revive Orthodox youth activities which have been somewhat lagging in the last decade. Let "Syndesmos" fulfill its mission in this country also, and plant the humble seeds without which no big plant can ever grow.

March, 1984

The Privilege of Freedom

A Russian bishop and theologian who recently visited the United States, Archbishop Basil Krivosheine, has publicly stated that, in his estimation, the autocephalous Orthodox Church in America is the only local Orthodox Church truly independent of the State and from political pressures and therefore free to organize its life in accordance with the truth of the Gospel and Orthodox tradition.

Once again we will be able to exercise this freedom in the fall at the All-American Council, which will meet in Montreal, Canada, October 25-28, 1977. Probably the most responsible act that will be taken at this Council will be the election of a new Metropolitan, since on October 25, the first day of the Council, the resignation of Metropolitan Ireney, will become effective.

In many ways this election will be ground-breaking. For the first time our Church will elect its Primate as an autocephalous Church, since His Beatitude Metropolitan Ireney had been already the head of the former Russian Metropolia at the time when the autocephaly was granted. With wisdom, patience and unpretentiousness, he guided our Church through a historic, transitional period. But now we stand at a new threshold. Remarkable progress was achieved during Metropolitan Ireney's tenure, including the entrance into our Church of several national groups which were seeking Orthodox unity and common witness. For the first time they will now take full part in the election of the new Primate, who will be called upon to symbolize the pluralistic, missionary and forward-looking calling of our Church. Fortunately, the foundation of our mission has been laid long ago. Early in this century, Archbishop Tikhon conceived his

147

vision of a united, multi-ethnic and autocephalous American Church (1905) and thus defined the role of the Russian Church in this country not in terms of ethnic, "phyletistic" self-affirmation, but as a mission to all Americans.

The election of the Metropolitan will take place according to the canons, giving to the entire body of the Church—clergy and laity alike—the opportunity of selecting the candidates, while preserving the Holy Synod's right to canonical sanction. Unfortunately, nowhere else in the contemporary Orthodox world does there exist the possibility for the Church to express its nature, its God-established structure as freely and as fully.

Shall we live up to this privilege of freedom?

June, 1977

Bishops, Clergy and Laity

The procedure for the election of the new metropolitan of the Orthodox Church in America includes two stages. In a first ballot the delegates will be asked to name one single candidate: a bishop, an unmarried or widowed priest, or a theologically educated layman—any Orthodox Christian, canonically eligible for the episcopate. If a candidate receives two-thirds of the votes, his single name is presented to the members of the Holy Synod for their confirmation: their role is to confirm the candidate's Orthodox faith and canonical credentials, and to give their apostolic sanction by officially electing him as head of the Church.

The rationale behind this first ballot is to indicate whether an obvious and unquestionable candidate for the Metropolitanate is to be acknowledged by all in full unity of spirit.

If no one receives the two-thirds majority on the first ballot, the delegates will be called to vote again, placing two names on their ballots. The two candidates receiving the greatest number of votes will then be presented to the members of the Holy Synod, who will be free to choose either one of them by majority vote. (According to the Statute of the OCA, only ruling bishops have voting rights in the Synod.) The installation of the new metropolitan will follow their decision immediately.

This procedure of election expresses the basic truths of the Orthodox conception of the Church. First of all, it affirms that the Church is not made up only of bishops and priests, but that the Body of Christ includes all those who, in Baptism and Chrismation, have confessed the true faith and have committed themselves to God's saving will. The participation

149

of the entire body of the laity in the election of bishops is witnessed since the very early days of the Church, although it has not always been practiced in times when the Church did not enjoy its entire freedom. It is our distinct privilege and responsibility to be able to restore and affirm this important privilege of all the Orthodox Christians.

However, this procedure for the election of the new metropolitan will also acknowledge that the Church is not a democracy in the worldly sense of this word: in the Church we are called to manifest the will of God, not the will of the "people." Certainly, God speaks through His people also, but only if this people follows the principles and rules (or "canons") establishing an apostolic order. In the preservation of this order, the bishops, successors of the apostles, have a decisive responsibility: all of them will be personally judged on the Last Day for the way in which they remained faithful to their calling, but they have no right to renounce it now. Their task is not to exercise lordship over the people (Christ said: "The kings of the Gentiles exercise lordship over them: but not so with you" (Luke 22:25-26), but to recognize, to discern the will of God when it comes from the people, while also guiding and feeding the flock away from sin and evil.

Only if this spirit will truly prevail at the Council in Montreal will the election also be to the glory of God and serve the prospering of the Orthodox Church in this country.

September, 1977

The New Metropolitan

In the Orthodox doctrine of the Church, there exist only three ranks of sacramental ministry: the bishop, the priest and the deacon. Among the other titles used by members of the clergy, some have become purely honorary, others reflect a function of leadership necessary for the progress and the good order of the Church. These titles have frequently changed in history and still differ today in the usage of the various local Orthodox Churches. The title of "patriarch" is adopted by some Orthodox primates, but it does not provide its incumbent with any special power and reflects only the element of prestige which belongs to some ancient and historically glorious episcopal sees.

What is a constant and necessary element in the life of every autonomous or autocephalous church—whatever titles are otherwise used to designate its leadership—is the "Synod," or council of diocesan bishops, meeting periodically to consecrate new bishops, to solve controversies, to secure the unity and good order of the entire Church. The Synod requires a permanent chairman who is obligatorily one of the bishops in charge of one of the dioceses and holds, among his peers, the position of "first among equals," with certain clearly defined prerogatives of leadership and initiative. The title of "metropolitan" is among the most ancient and traditional of all: already in the fourth century it was used to designate the bishop of the major city (metropolis) of the area at a time when there were not yet any "patriarchs" or "archbishops" at all in the Church.

In ancient times, a metropolitan was elected by the clergy and laity of his own diocese (as were all the other bishops). However, the Statute of the Orthodox Church in America involves the entire Church, i.e., all the dioceses, in the elective process, thus giving the metropolitan wider prestige. Fundamentally, however, he is nothing more than the chairman of the Synod and the "first among equal" bishops of the Church. According to the canons of the Apostles, he cannot act in general Church affairs without the approval of the other bishops and, reciprocally, they cannot act in any way without him.

These general principles of Church organization must be well understood by all, especially by the delegates at the All-American Council in Montreal who will participate in the election. The system of conciliarity—the very basis of the Orthodox doctrine of the Church—excludes the possibility of a metropolitan who would act dictatorially and assume full personal power in administering the Church. The canonical structure of individual dioceses and the participation of all in sharing responsibility for the life of the Church, as determined by the Statute, are sufficient guarantees against primatial despotism. They only require that a metropolitan speak on behalf of the Church, represent it in the outside world, manifest its vision and its goal: the unity of Orthodoxy in America, its missionary expansion, its witness on the ecumenical and social scenes, in total faithfulness to the Word of God and the tradition of the Councils and the Fathers.

The internal life and administrative structure of the Church has been relatively well oiled and stabilized during the tenure of Metropolitan Ireney. It is unlikely that it will suffer substantial changes under his successor, whoever he may be. But the image of the Orthodox Church in America, as it is being watched by our own faithful as well as by outsiders, will certainly depend upon the choice made in Montreal. May the Holy Spirit guide us with His power and wisdom!

October, 1977

For Many Years!

It is very easy to see that the election of His Beatitude, Metropolitan Theodosius, as Primate of the Orthodox Church in America, begins a new page in the history of our Church in this country. However, it is also quite important to discern the message of true spiritual maturity which comes from the Council in Montreal.

First of all, it was a Council much better attended than the previous ones with the presence of hundreds of observers added to the 463 voting delegates. It was also a council where the various ethnic groups were united at all levels in service to the One Church, proving that such unity is possible without loss of anyone's identity, thus prefiguring authentic Orthodox unity in this country. Finally, the interaction of the various ministries and responsibilities were put to a successful test. As these columns have often emphasized, the true nature of the Church cannot be defined in terms of either exclusive power of the bishops, or domination of the laity by the priest, or in terms of "popular democracy."

The clear will of the Church, as a body, was overwhelmingly indicated in the two successive ballots: this Church is ready to assume a mission to America and does not want to remain a purely immigrant church. This solemn affirmation, however, came not as a revolution, but as a reaffirmation of a principle enunciated one hundred and ten years ago by the first Orthodox bishop in America, St Innocent, whose letter, written in 1867, was read while the delegates were waiting for the results of the second ballot. More than a century ago St Innocent understood that if the Orthodox Church was to make progress—or even survive— in this country, it must open its doors to all Americans without forcing anyone to use a language in worship which is foreign to him or her. Even if our own Synod of Bishops wanted to resist that affirmation, they could not do so because of the results of the two ballots. Our bishops, however, possessed the freedom and the responsibility to choose between the two top candidates. And it is, indeed, wise that this choice was left to them, since the vast majority of the delegates were not in a position to pass judgment on the personal qualities of the candidates whom they did not really know. And, of course, the bishops, by virtue of their office, legitimately hold the last say in every Church matter, and particularly in the election of their peers, because bishops are ultimately elects of God, 'not of men.

So, let us wish our new metropolitan "many years." Since he is still quite a young man, our wish and our prayer is likely to become a reality. For several decades to come, Metropolitan Theodosius will have the opportunity and the mission to fulfill the mandate received in Montreal: to work for Orthodox unity, to emphasize the missionary dimension of the Church, to preside over the growth and expansion of Orthodoxy in this country. He needs our help, our prayers and our love.

December, 1977

Ethnicity

One of the notable phenomena of the American social scene has been, in the last two or three years, a revival of concern for "ethnicity." The "black power" movement has spurred other "powers"—Italian, Polish, Greek, Ukrainian, Russian—to rise to the defense of their identity against the prevailing melting-pot of "Wasp" culture. This new sense of ethnic identity may indeed bring positive results: a new sense of human dignity and responsibility in the black American community; the preservation of old cultural treasures among American Indians; the development of inborn qualities among ethnic minorities that were frequently ghettoized and remained away from the mainstream of social development.

However, the new emphasis on "ethnicity" is not without dangers. It may contribute to preserve the ghettos. It may give an illusion of identity to minority groups whose actual ties with cultures, other than the American, are quite superficial. To preserve "Russian culture," for example, one has to know more than a few Russian dances and a few incomprehensible Slavonic words of church prayers: one has to be initiated to a whole complex of cultural factors which can, in the long run, be validly preserved and fruitfully developed only in Russia. There is nothing wrong in trying to preserve, for emotional and sentimental reasons, even these little superficial bits of one's ethnic origin, but it is an illusion to believe that they can alone nourish the cultural requirements of twentieth-century American-born man or woman. These requirements will necessarily be met only in the American school and the American university.

And finally, the Church cannot and should not be identified with "ethnicity," unless she also is to be reduced to these superficial "cultural" remnants and lose all existential value for both the old and the young. The Orthodox Church has always been a people's Church. It has deep roots in the cultural identity of the various nations of Eastern Europe. It was natural that, in the early stages of immigration history, she should be the rallying point for the immigrants. However, she cannot be reduced to that social function. She has a missionary responsibility for all men. She can never identify herself with either a political ideology or an ethnic group. The Orthodox are unanimous in denouncing the western promoters of Christian "secularism," which reduces Christianity to social causes, but they themselves do the same whenever they use the Church as a mere tool for the preservation of illusory ethnic interests.

Let us respect and cultivate everything which is precious in our ethnic cultures. But let us also remember that the Church is not an instrument or tool for earthly causes, but a foretaste of God's kingdom for all men.

June-July, 1972

Whose Church?

One of the essential points in the Orthodox understanding of the Church is that no individual, no group, no organization can monopolize power and authority on any level of Church life. The Church is Christ's Body and all power and authority are His. We, the members of the Body, are called to fulfill our functions and our responsibilities in our respective positions, some important and some less important. But we cannot break the common life of the whole Body and pursue the particular interests of the "clergy," of the "bishops," of the "laity," or of our parish without losing sight of what the Church is all about.

Of course, the history of the Church has known many bad bishops, bad priests and bad laymen. For example, in 1596 the majority of the bishops of the Kievan Metropolia joined the "Unia" with Rome and Orthodoxy was saved by laymen who organized themselves into brotherhoods, bought the churches back from illegitimate owners and finally rebuilt the Body of the Church which had been made headless through the betrayal of its leaders. At other, more normal times, bishops alone gathered in Ecumenical or local councils, defended the faith and defined Orthodoxy. The Church has always condemned, as sectarian and heeretical, those groups who thought that the sacramental hierarchical structure of the Church was not the only real pattern of its internal organization.

But this fight of laymen against apostate bishops, and these condemnations by episcopal assemblies of lay sectarians, were in the name of Christ's Truth and Christ's Church alone, and not in order to defend the laymen's "rights," or the bishops' "power." In the Orthodox Church everyone, at all times, has the right, and even the obligation, to speak out and to act in any circumstances, and before anybody, on behalf of Christ's Truth. This is the freedom and the responsibility that we all enjoy as Orthodox Christians. And it is a real shame that sometimes, instead of being logical with ourselves, with our own Christian dignity, we mistakenly think that a civil court is more able to secure our "rights" than obedience to God's law, which we often simply do not care to learn or understand.

However, if Orthodoxy is to flourish and to expand in America, it will be only if we ourselves, as well as those who look at us from outside, will see in our Church—the True Church of God.

December, 1965

Responsibility

In the person of Metropolitan Leonty, the Church has lost a leader who was a living incarnation of our links with the past and a holy witness of what we mostly need in the future: a responsible and total devotion to the Church as such, to the prosperity of Orthodoxy in America, and not to any human interest, however valuable in itself.

This spirit of responsibility must prevail among us during this period of transition.

Our Church in America is one of the rare units of the universal Orthodox Church where the election of bishops takes place with the participation of the whole body of the faithful. Practically everywhere else, new primates—patriarchs, archbishops, metropolitans—are elected by the bishops alone. We have, however, the great privilege of living in accordance with the decisions of the historic Moscow Sobor of 1917-1918, which restored the ancient Christian principle of giving to *every member of the Church* a share of responsibility of the life of the Church as a whole.

But let us remember that this responsibility implies that we are not children, but adults in Christ; that we have a vision of the Church's needs; that we know exactly what is involved in the choice we are going to make. As members of our parishes, when we elect our representatives to the Sobor, as Sobor-members, when we cast our ballots—we are entrusted with the responsibility for the Body of Christ itself, His Holy Church.

It is not a time to tremble a little, but, first of all, to pray and to think?

Of course, the continuity of the Church's existence is guaranteed by the Apostolic succession of the episcopate.

Our choice will have to be confirmed by the bishops, and if we fail to express our choice clearly, the bishops will make the choice for us. But let us all realize that God will give us a unique opportunity to become His spokesmen, to express His will. And His will is certainly that the primate of the Church be a leader, a guide, an example on the way to salvation, a teacher of our generation and of our children, a spokesman for Orthodoxy before the world of today.

Let us not fail in our responsibility!

June-July, 1965

The Bishop and the Church

For reasons which are impossible to enumerate here, there is, in many minds, a great confusion concerning the episcopal office in the Church.

In the early years of Christianity, in the times of the Councils and of the Fathers, the bishop was the center of the entire church life: his flock knew him as its Father, its Teacher, its Priest. Nothing in the Church was done without his knowledge, and he himself knew his people by name and understood his office not as an opportunity to exercise power, but, first of all, as a service—just as the Lord showed Himself to be the Servant. . . . It is for this service that Apostolic authority is also given to the bishop, and there can be no Church without him being the Pastor and the Head.

Today in America we often lose this conception of episcopacy. Instead of seeing in the Bishop the Teacher of the Apostolic faith, we visualize him as simply the occasion of a more elaborate—and often incomprehensible—liturgical ceremonial. Forgetting that it is in his name only that our parish priest can serve the Divine Liturgy, we are sometimes afraid of his "interventions" in our parish affairs, which we wrongly consider as "our own," and not God's. We do not understand where our money goes when it is being sent to the diocesan or the Metropolia's treasury, for we do not see any use for these institutions anyway. And finally, the shameful multiplicity of "jurisdictions" makes us feel that bishops are rather a divisive element in Church life, and we tend simply to forget that the most important character of episcopacy is to keep the Church *in unity* in every place.

Again, it is not the place here to look for responsibilities: everyone—bishops, priests, laymen—have their share in them.

But let us rather be concerned with the means to correct a situation both unusual and critical. The forthcoming Sobor gives us a crucial opportunity to make a decisive step *all together.*

The late Metropolitan Leonty had succeeded in preserving throughout the most difficult period of our Church's history a *holy* image of the episcopate. His successor's most difficult task will be to maintain that image. But he will also have to lead the Church in a different historical period: a period of further transition towards the establishment and progress of American Orthodoxy, a period of growth, of unification, of challege by both an increasingly secularized world and changing patterns of life.

We can be sure that whoever will be elected will receive the help and the guidance of the Holy Spirit. But let us also remember what Saint Leo the Great, a great Church Father, once said: "There is no greater sin than to bestow the grace of the Holy Spirit upon an unqualified person." And much of our troubles do come precisely from the fact that Saint Leo's precept has not been taken seriously enough in the past. The power of grace is not magic; to be effective, it requires the cooperation of man, and the Sobor will be the moment when we, all together, will have to designate the one who will be capable of giving that cooperation which *God needs today.*

August-September, 1965

Tradition and Traditions

The Orthodox Church is certainly the Church of Tradition. It holds that since the day of Pentecost and until the end of time the Holy Spirit guides the Church in all Truth, that it always remains essentially the same; in other words that the Church is always the same Church, maintaining the same apostolic message.

However, this Holy Tradition is not a dead, frozen deposit, but a continuous and full vision of God in which each human being—and also each culture, each nation—participates in its own particular way.

Living Tradition supposes a variety of local, human traditions, which all stand under the judgment of the One Catholic Truth: they are legitimate and fruitful as long as they conform to It and do not exclude other legitimate expressions of the same Orthodoxy.

The Orthodox Church in America, as we all experience it, grows out of a variety of local traditions, representing originally not only separate nations, but even national sub-divisions: "high-Russians," "Carpatho-Russians," "Galicians," seeking to preserve their identity—side by side with Greeks, Syrians, Romanians and Serbs. The unified American Church of the future will only gain if it adopts the positive elements of each one, creatively adapting them to her needs .

The vast majority of "Russian Orthodox" Americans are connected with the branches of Eastern Christianity which for many centuries heroically preserved the Orthodox faith in the Roman Catholic Austro-Hungarian Empire. Forced into "union" with Rome, they were ultimately guided by a Naumovich or a Toft back to Orthodoxy. At the moment of their massive return, the Church was faced by the respon-

sibility of bringing them into true Orthodoxy and, therefore,
liberating them from the remnants of the hated "latiniza-
tion," encouraging them to preserve and develop their an-
cestral Orthodox piety. In this process of adaptation, mistakes were sometimes made: the beautiful and authentically
Orthodox custom of corporate chanting was replaced (fortunately, not everywhere), by choirs of classical Russian
type; embittered controversies sometimes raged over minor
issues, such as the form of priests' vestments. And because
the essential was not separated from the secondary, those who
in general desired to preserve the traditions of their fore-
fathers began to resist changes where they were really
necessary.

Today the Church of America approaches its maturity.
It is therefore necessary for all to settle the pending problems not in the light of the quarrels of the past, but exclusively on the basis of Orthodoxy: problems such as the
celebration of several liturgies by one single priest on the
same altar on the same day, or baptism by sprinkling, involve the faith itself and must be solved as such. Without
any excessive formalism or self-righteousness, making all possible accommodations, we must keep our Orthodoxy orthodox
and not preserve in our own parishes the "latinisms" which
are now sometimes rejected by Rome itself and which will
certainly never fit into an Orthodox understanding of the
Church.

However, whatever needs to be done is to be done in
the name of Truth, and not to make one local or national
tradition triumph over another: all human "customs" and
"practices" are to be confronted not with each other, but
with the Tradition of the One Orthodox Catholic Church.

February, 1966

The F.R.O.C.

The annual convention of the Federated Russian Orthodox Clubs, held at the Waldorf-Astoria Hotel in New York
city during the Labor Day weekend, was in many ways symbolic of the present shape of the organization: its "status,"
its achievements and its problems.

As an honorary member, who was also honored with
the opportunity of addressing the convention on behalf of
St Vladimir's Seminary, I am fully aware of the very positive
and progressive role played by the F.R.O.C. during the past
decades of Orthodoxy's history in America, and I sincerely
wish that this role be continued also in the future. It is
this awareness and this wish which lead me to use this
editorial column for a brief comment on the issue of the
relationship between the F.R.O.C. and the Church.

In past years, this issue has been a burning one in almost
all the chapters. On several occasions the "Russian Orthodox
Journal" has devoted controversial articles to it. The officers
of the F.R.O.C. have often mentioned it, orally and in writing, as an issue which needs discussion. After all this, one
would expect—from an organization which has placed so
much emphasis on democratic procedure—a thorough debate of
the issue on the convention floor and some sort of conclusion.

However, the two attempts at starting such a debate met
with the fierce opposition of several former and present
leaders of the organization. These leaders succeeded in tabling
all motions, even though they had only a tentative and
exploratory character, which could lead to a solution. The
ambiguous issue of Church-F.R.O.C. relationships will therefore continue to poison the atmosphere, not only inside the
organization, but also in inter-Orthodox or ecumenical circles—

such as C.E.O.Y.L.A. or the National Council of Churches.

Meanwhile, it is quite obvious that the dilemma—to be "in the Church" or to be "independent"—is a false one. An overwhelming majority of the convention members, as well as of the entire F.R.O.C. constituency, is composed of faithful Orthodox Christians who, through their parishes, are also regular members of the Russian Orthodox Greek Catholic Church of America. It is therefore only by a misunderstanding that fears of of hierarchical "control" and of "clericalism" prevent the official integration of the F.R.O.C. in the overall Church organization. If "freedom" is threatened by Church membership, this freedom already has been surrendered by the F.R.O.C. members by their belonging to Orthodox parishes.

If, however, Church membership is first of all a responsibility, then the F.R.O.C. is called upon to assume, as an organization, the role which belongs to the Orthodox laity as a whole: to shape the present and the future of the Church, to speak for the Church to those who are outside of it, and to fight—with a freedom which belongs to every Orthodox Christian—against anything which contradicts the Gospel of Christ.

To become officially a lay organization of the Church is a responsibility and a privilege—certainly not a bond.

October, 1967

The Church: One Body

A friend complained to me recently about the weakness of our Church's public relations. The last Sobor ended without press releases and public announcements. The central governing body of the second largest Orthodox jurisdiction met in New York without being noticed by the secular press and its decisions will have to reach its own constituency, as well as other interested parties, through the more esoteric channels of the Orthodox press.

It may indeed be the case that public relations has not been the strongest department of our Church. One wonders, however, whether this is really a weakness or a sign which stands in healthy contrast to the cheap commercialism of much of American religion today: controversial statements that make headlines but misguide people; self-congratulations that cover spiritual emptiness; statistics and bureaucracy that replace pastoral care and guidance. While avoiding all this, the Sobor witnessed a major spiritual and psychological event: the unanimous adoption of a healthy and balanced definition of our parish structure.

During the last decade this issue was poisoned with several fundamental misconceptions of Orthodox Church life: the opposition between the "material" and the "spiritual" in parish life; the fear that the clergy were aspiring to control parish property; the idea that the spiritual leadership of the priest was incompatible with the full participation and responsibility of the layman in parish life. The unanimous vote on the new parish statute shows that mutual trust has been restored and strengthened; that the Church is indeed one Body.

The task which lies ahead is to build the Orthodox

Church of America upon an 'infra-structure" now solidly laid; to interpret to those who do not understand it what is obviously the only possible Orthodox solution of the parish problem; to provide the Church with priests able to teach, to explain and to guide. This last objective is particularly important because the priest's task and responsibility are incredibly difficult. Our Church is privileged to have at its disposal for the preparation of its priests a formally accredited graduate school—St Vladimir's Seminary—and a school now seeking undergraduate accreditation—St Tikhon's. Hopefully, together these two schools will contribute a full cycle of theological studies. Coordinated with each other, yet each keeping its own particular tradition and distinct purpose—one as an undergraduate and the other as a graduate school—they should be able to provide our Church with well-trained priests for the future.

With many obstacles still unavoidably before us, our Church has been placed, by the last Sobor, on the road of fruitful progress and articulate development.

January, 1968

American Responsibility

The forthcoming Second Council of the Orthodox Church in America, convened especially in order to discuss and eventually adopt a new Statute for the entire Church, will meet on October 19-21 at St Tikhon's Monastery. The draft, prepared by a special commission, has been widely distributed; preliminary suggestions for changes and emendations have been received and will be taken into consideration; all parishes, priests, parish officers and future delegates to the Council still have the time to get acquainted with the text, if they have not as yet done so. When the Council convenes, everyone will have had an opportunity to do his homework and should be able to cooperate responsibly in the big Church event, involving, according to our Orthodox teaching, not only our human efforts, but the active and guiding power of the Holy Spirit.

The Church is not simply a democratic corporation, adopting by-laws, providing occasions for parliamentary debates, and settling disputes by majority vote: it is the living organism of the Body of Christ, in which bishops, priests, laymen, men, women, young and old have their particular role and function. Almost everywhere in the world, the normal functioning of this organism is being limited by external circumstances or improper limitations: in Communist countries, the State prevents the free expression of opinions; in many other churches, including some major Orthodox jurisdictions in this country, the clergy and laity have no voice at all in the selection of candidates for episcopacy or in settling their own ecclesiastical destiny.

It is therefore the fate and responsibility of the Orthodox Church in America to use all the opportunities given to it by Divine Providence. The aim of the Statute is precisely to define the responsibility of everyone in building up the body of the Church.

The new draft is not very different from the statute of the Metropolia as it existed before the autocephaly. It only tries to take full account of our now canonical situation as an autocephalous Church—a Church which is open to all Orthodox Americans, whatever their ethnic background. It also further clarifies those issues which were often discussed in the past: respective rights and duties of clergy and laity, parish property, ecclesiastical courts, etc.

The Council also will have to give serious consideration to the fact that the Church cannot fulfill its new mission, with national and international responsibilities, without an appropriate staff and an appropriate budget. Acceptable priorities between parish, diocesan and national spending will have to be defined. The Statute will define our common goals and, all together, we will have to live up to them.

October, 1971

Parish Property

The question of parish property remains, surprisingly, quite a hot issue in some Orthodox communities in America. In particular, it is being said that the bishops of the Orthodox Church in America are claiming the control of parish property. Rumors of that nature are being spread by people who are either ignorant of the facts, or are maliciously interested in Church strife and disunity.

The Statute of the former Metropolia, now the Orthodox Church in America, is perfectly clear on this point. Its article VI, paragraph 12, states: "*The parish corporation is the sole owner of all parish property, assets and funds.*" It is quite important that every time the question of parish property is raised this sentence be brought to the attention of those who deny the evidence.

The only limitation to this right of property is the spiritual goals of the parish itself. The same articles continues: "In administering them (i.e., the parish property, assets and funds), the parishioners and the officers elected by them must always remember the religious nature, purposes and goals of the parish and act as trustees of God's, and not man's property. The parish, as the whole Church, serves God and cares for God's work in the world, and all decisions concerning parish property must be inspired by that care and by the spiritual needs of the Church."

The same principles are being retained and clarified in the draft Statute which is presently being distributed to all parishes for their discussion, so that their delegates at the forthcoming Council in October may adopt it, after presenting all the amendments which they consider necessary. All necessary clarifications are available. Debates and discussions are welcome.

The future of our Church life requires a uniform Statute for the entire Church. This will secure the proper operation of the organs of Church administration at all levels: parish, diocese, national Church. Suspicions and misunderstandings must be overcome; slander and adventurism eliminated. The by-laws of individual parishes must be in conformity with the Statute, so that each parish may be entitled to all its rights—regular appointment of priests, appropriate representation at diocesan assemblies and All-American Councils—while also fulfilling its responsibilities towards the life of the entire Church. These should be our goals for the forthcoming months.

April, 1971

Common Talk on New Statute

The October council of the Orthodox Church in America, after the adoption of a brief Constitution—an action required by the new canonical status of the Church—had also decided to hold another special session in October 1971 to discuss and adopt a new Statute, i.e., a set of detailed by-laws which will define the rights and duties of all our ecclesiastical organizations on the national, the diocesan and the parish levels.

Actually, the new Statute will not contain anything revolutionary: the Metropolia had existed for almost fifty years as a de facto autocephalous Church, and its present Statute reflects this situation. What is now needed is more clarity in several sections of the Statute—a clearer definition of the proper responsibility of diocesan structures, for example—and, especially, an appropriate response to the need for becoming the Church for all Orthodox Americans, and not only for those of Russian background.

The Holy Synod, at a joint session with the Metropolitan Council, has appointed a committee of clergy and laity to work on the revision of the Statute. The results of the committee's work are being checked by the Canonical Department (Archbishop Valerian, chairman). The Metropolitan Council and the Synod at their current sessions (February and March) will also look into the draft. They will not be called upon to endorse it, however, but only to approve its distribution to the parishes.

During the six months before the session of the Council next October, every parish council will have an opportunity to discuss the text, to ask questions, to clear misunderstandings and to make changes, so that the vote of the Council may be a fully conscious one. It is extremely important to make sure that the discussion of the draft in the parishes takes place freely, responsibly and without delay. The priests and the lay officials of each parish must be equally concerned with securing the best way of clearing up the misunderstandings of the past.

The Church is Christ's Church. We are all members. Church work can succeed only as a common task.

February, 1971

The New Statute

After a careful reading of a draft, prepared by a special commission, the Council of the Orthodox Church in America adopted the Statute which will now regulate the life of the entire Church. Actually, the new Statute is not really "new"; it represents an attempt to apply the Orthodox teachings about the Church to the concrete realities of our time. It uses the principles of the ancient Orthodox canon law and translates them into a language directly understandable by those who are responsible for the life of our Church on the central, diocesan and parochial levels. Every priest, every parish committee member and every responsible parishioner should acquaint himself with the text, which has now been adopted by the highest administrative authority of our Church and sanctioned by the supreme authority of the Holy Synod.

The basic principle which underlines the whole text is that the Church is a *single body*: no member of the body can live in isolation from, and even less, in opposition to the other members. Inside the body, however, there is a diversity of functions and responsibilities. The bishops, for example, are particularly responsible for the purity of faith, and the priests are their representatives in each parish. Since the faith is indeed the source and the goal of Church life, there is no true Orthodoxy without every latitude being given to the bishops and the priests to exercise their ministry *in all aspects* of life of the dioceses and the parishes.

Of course, no one in the Church is personally infallible—and certainly not the clergy. We Orthodox also believe that the entire people of God, clergy and laity, are responsible for keeping the faith, as well as for the entire life of the Church. Every Church function is exercised in the community and for the community. The Lord Jesus Himself described the sharp contrast which exists between authority as it is exercised "in the world" and the type of authority which He wanted among His disciples: "You know that the rulers of the Gentiles lord it over them, and their great men exercise authority over them. It shall not be so among you: but whoever would be great among you must be your servant... even as the Son of man came not to be served but to serve, and to give his life as a ransom for many" (Mtt 25:25-28).

Only that authority will be authentic and justified which is rooted in service. In the Church the only "privilege" is to serve God and fellow-men. Whenever anybody—either among the clergy or among the laity—desires "to be served," he loses all his moral rights and privileges and, in fact, betrays his Christian vocation.

This is the only valid approach to the sections of the Statute describing the various functions of the Church. Even if some of these descriptions may still seem imperfect and will need further improvements at later councils, let us remember that the effectiveness of the Statute will ultimately depend upon the spirit with which the texts will be understood and applied. A healthy Church life will be impossible whenever there will be no mutual trust and no unity of purpose.

Both trust and purpose were living realities during the Council in the midst of discussions which were at times quite heated. Our entire Church has shown a remarkable maturity of judgment during the Council. Let us hope and pray that this same spirit will continue to preside over it during the trying years to come.

November, 1971

Electing a Bishop

The forthcoming election of a bishop for one of the largest dioceses of the Orthodox Church in America is an opportunity for reflecting upon the extraordinary responsibility involved in this canonical act.

Whatever procedure one adopts—and procedures have varied in history—it is the faith of the Church that the election reflects a divine choice and is actually performed not only by man, but also by the Holy Spirit. The Church is not a human organization, ruled by any of the systems which man may devise—democracy, autocracy, clergy-rule or laity-rule—but a temple of God, where God and man meet, where man is being led to eternal life, where God, in His mercy, gives to men and women the privilege of being His sons and daughters.

It is this new dignity, which man acquires in the Church, that also allows him to share mysteriously in the acts of divine choice. Holy Scripture teaches us that the ministries of the Church—and especially the ministries responsible for the performance of sacraments, for the maintenance of the true faith, for the unity of the Church—are gifts of the Holy Spirit. However, because the Church is the Body of Christ, because all of us clergy and laity—are members of the Body, we are all called to participate in the selection of those who are invested with this grace of the Holy Spirit: "It has seemed good to the Holy Spirit and to us" (Acts 15:23).

According to the Statute of our Church, candidates for the episcopal office are nominated by the diocesan assemblies and then canonically elected and consecrated by the other bishops. This procedure is exactly the one which is described as the normal one by the early Fathers of the Church (for

example, St Hippolytus in the third century) and is taken
for granted by the canons. However, it has not been always
followed in the later course of history. With the establishment of Christianity as a state religion, laity and lower clergy
have been gradually excluded from participation in the elec-
tions. State authorities have interfered in the choice of candidates (although these interventions are strictly forbidden
by canon law). The participation of clergy and laity in the
election of bishops had been officially restored by the Council
of Moscow (1917-1918) for the Russian Church, but the
revolutionary events which followed did not allow its im-
plementation after 1922. In today's Orthodoxy our Church
is practically the only one where the original Christian norm
for selecting bishops is being implemented.

This places upon us an extraordinary responsibility. We
participate in a Church act where the guidance of the Holy
Spirit is to be heard and followed. It would be a blasphemy,
for example, to bestow the episcopal office upon someone
who would be unable to live up to it (and such blasphemies
have taken place in the past!). Hence the requirements concerning the theological education, the moral standards and
other qualifications of the candidates, which should conform to the standards inherited from Holy Tradition, existing
in the Orthodox Church throughout the world and also
required by the episcopal office to be exercised in twentieth-
century America.

Not only the Diocese of Pittsburgh, but the entire Church
will pray so that the right candidate be nominated by clergy
and laity of Western Pennsylvania, and that the Holy Synod
of our Bishops, exercising the highest pastoral office with
wisdom and, if necessary, with discernment, may give the
ultimate and final sanction to the election.

April, 1972

Growing Maturity

The Third All-American Council of the Orthodox Church in America did not face any of the burning issues which dominated the previous meetings at St Tikhon's in 1970 and 1971—acceptance of autocephaly and adoption of new statutes—but it was a remarkable show of growing maturity and renewed dedication to the work ahead.

The problem of clergy-laity relations, seen as a conflict of "rights" and "privileges," which used to dominate the debates at previous Councils, was apparently quite outgrown. Mutual confidence was strengthened by the presence of a new generation of both priests and laymen. I was personally quite struck by the number of new, young delegates, well-informed, active and responsible. The organization of the Council, including sectional meetings and workshops, gave a greater opportunity for everyone to express his views and participate in the general discussion, which at plenary sessions is inevitably monopolized by only a few. This constructive spirit which dominated the Council led to serious decisions.

Whether the financial crisis will be overcome or not depends entirely on the ability of the delegates to impress the urgency of the matter upon their parishes. The truly remarkable enthusiasm which embraced the Council at the last session is a good sign for the future. Much will also depend on the ability of the Central Church Administration to communicate with dioceses and the parishes, which deserve to receive a constant flow of information about what is being done by the Church-at-large. The Council itself was a success in this area: many delegates expressed their astonishment at seeing the exhibits on the educational and missionary activities conducted by the Church in so many areas—and about which they knew nothing. Let us hope that the new Chancellor, Fr Daniel Hubiak, and the other officers, who will be appointed shortly to work under his direction, will receive the means and the cooperation of all to carry on the work of the Church.

Considering the critical conditions under which Orthodox Churches live in many parts of the world, the political passions which divide them in Greece and the Middle East, the legal limitations which they suffer in Communist countries, the members of the Council became aware once more of the amazing possibilities which are open before the Orthodox Church in America. Gathering exery morning and every evening in the chapel, participating in great numbers in the Mysteries of Confession and Holy Communion, they received a new vision of the Church of which they are members, a new power to transcend their human limitations to become truly one in Christ.

December, 1973

Our Privilege

An Orthodox Bishop from Europe, Archbishop Basil of Brussels, learned theologian and a defender of Alexander Solzhenitsyn—even though he belongs to the jurisdiction of the Moscow patriarchate—participated in an international theological conference held at St Vladimir's Seminary in 1971. Asked to give his impressions at the concluding banquet, he said: "I enjoyed being here because, among all the Orthodox Churches of the world, the autocephalous Orthodox Church in America is the only one which is totally independent of the State."

This statement of Archbishop Basil is true: in no other country today does there exist a total freedom of the Orthodox Church to elect its bishops and other leaders, to express freely its views on the issues of the day, to determine the conditions of its life and activities. We wish that all Orthodox Americans were able to share with us this freedom, which is in conformity with the canons of the Church and, we believe, with the will of God for His entire people.

The All-American Councils are the main expressions of this authentic freedom of our Church. The delegates meeting this November in Cleveland, Ohio, are called upon to exercise it not only with dynamism and wisdom, but also with a "churchly" spirit. Church councils are not identical with democratic assemblies; they are the expressions of the Church itself. In the Church we are not alone, since Christ Himself, the Head of the Church, is in our midst. He is the One whose will we seek to accomplish. He is the One who determines the internal structures which make the Church to be the Church: bishops, priests, deacons, lay men and women, forming a single body, invested with particular responsibilities, free, but also responsible to God.

The control which the State—i.e., the powers of the secular world—exercises over the Church in so many countries is contrary to the very nature of the Church. Our brothers who are under such control cannot do much about it: we should not condemn them in any way. Our obligation is to remain true to the remarkable privilege of freedom which has been granted to us. For our freedom from the State does not mean automatically that we are also free from other means by which the "world" enslaves us: nationalism, divisiveness, money, success-seeking, etc.

Let us pray for the Council of Cleveland: let it be a new liberating event at which, using our own privilege fully, we make a decisive contribution to the spiritual and missionary growth of Orthodoxy in America.

October, 1975

Stewardship

A decision of the Metropolitan Council, confirmed by the Holy Synod, introduces a new principle in the financial policies of the Church: the principle of stewardship. So far, the very meager central budget was covered exclusively by the proceeds of minimal membership dues, identical for all adult members of the Church.

The reasons which motivated the decision and which will undoubtedly be also discussed at the next All-American Council in Montreal, Canada (October, 1977), lie, on the one hand, in the growing missionary, educational and administrative responsibilities faced by our central Church bodies, and, on the other hand, in deeper spiritual motivations.

This spiritual motivation, which has been recognized long ago by other religious bodies, is much more important than simple budgetary considerations.

Membership dues are a purely formal way of fulfilling an obligation. They are also basically unjust, since they remain the same for the rich and the poor: the executive who receives a high salary contributes the same amount as the senior citizen living on Social Security. Stewardship, meanwhile, implies a sense of responsibility for the life of the Church, awareness of its real needs and readiness to assume that part of the common burden that is proportionate to one's real possibilities. It is a free act of an adult and a responsible Christian.

Of course, the old system of dues will not be abandoned immediately. But as our Church grows not only in size, but also in Spirit, one should welcome the initiative taken by the Metropolitan Council and give it—in every diocese, where stewardship needs are being distributed in proportion to membership—overwhelming support.

December, 1976

The Church Gathers Together

Each All-American Council is an opportunity for the Church to come together and for all its members to understand anew the ways in which God wants us to go.

Here is an essential element of Orthodoxy: the Church is not made up of bishops alone, or of clergy, and it is not a democratic voluntary society. The Holy Spirit has been granted—and is still being granted—to all together, with each one exercising his or her ministry in the light of this unique gift.

There are, indeed, particular functions and responsibilities which belong to bishops, to priests, to deacons, to the laity. But whenever anyone attempts to exercise this responsibility in isolation from the whole Church, he or she cannot anymore pretend to a truly Orthodox ecclesial sense.

How often people have tried to reduce this mystery of togetherness to simple, rational, but inevitably unilateral formulas, forgetting that, in the Orthodox Church, power really belongs only to Christ, as the Head, and to the Spirit, as guiding us to Christ and the Father. All the ministries and responsibilities are valid only if they are determined by this need to discover and fulfill the will of God. And all those who are invested with the ministries—all of them, without exception—are sometimes tempted "to go it alone": bishops and priests to require obedience without explaining, teaching and, truly, loving their flocks; laity to adopt a defensive and mistrustful attitude towards the clergy.

Humanly speaking, such temptations are understandable. History, old and new, recalls many examples of bishops, priests, and laity not really deserving trust and obedience. But the solution is not to reject the Orthodox doctrine of the Church, but to uncover its very mystery, and to believe that if the Church has existed two thousand years, it is not because—at all times—she was composed of unworthy sinners, but because the Spirit of God has maintained her as the "pillar and foundation of Truth."

May, 1983

184

The All-American Council
Meets in Detroit

Our Church in America is governed by the All-American Council. In the framework of the Council, all members of the Church—bishops, clergy, laity—exercise their respective responsibilities and give answer to God and the Church for the way in which they fulfill their ministries and live their Christian lives.

I have met people saying that the forthcoming Council in Detroit is not likely to be as important as those which preceded it because there will be no election of a new metropolitan, no new statute to approve, no major issue to decide. Such comments show total misunderstanding of the most important privileges and duties of all of us: those which are permanent and unavoidable and, therefore, truly central to the life of the Church.

The *privileges* of those of us who will attend the Council will, first of all, consist

— in a living experience of the unity of the whole Church, realized in the Divine Liturgy, celebrated in common with so many men and women from all parts of the country;

— a living knowledge of the always enriching diversity of the life of our parishes, from which we can learn so much;

— a deeper awareness of the fact that our Church, since it was granted autocephaly ten years ago, has received in its fold many new people, and that it has "reached into the future" better than we sometimes realize;

— a concrete opportunity to discover achievements, as well as persistent deficiencies, in the activities of the various department of the Church, and to pass judgment on them all.

The *duty* of the participants will be to assume a fully responsible stewardship of the Church by defining possibilities and impossibilities, by giving advice and direction, by informing the respective parishes of its needs, and, hopefully, correcting its frightfully inadequate financial situation.

Those of us who will not be able to be in Detroit also have the privilege and the duty to make sure that our views and feelings are made known to our representatives and, later, to accept and to implement the Council decisions as decisions of the whole Church.

October, 1980

Growth and Mission

The theme of Church Growth, which—since the Council of Philadelphia—remains as the focal point of our national Church life, is clearly associated with the idea that the Church is missionary. Or, to put it more exactly, the emphasis on mission is the most important sign of real Church growth—a growth in the Spirit, as well as in numbers.

Although this might not be equally true everywhere, and in all the parishes, missionary awareness has grown significantly in our Church during the past years. Of course, this awareness is not really "new": even before 1918, the Diocese of North America was often designated as a "mission," and its pioneers prided themselves (legitimately) on being "missionaries." However, in those days their mission was primarily directed at Slavic immigrants. Today, and especially since the autocephaly of 1970, our Church is committed to spread the Orthodox faith for the benefit of all Americans, following the example of its earlier Alaskan founders, St Herman and St Innocent.

To many the commitment seems much too daring, and we do not always realize all its implications. The ridiculously small budget of the Department of Missions is certainly not illustrative of a missionary sense which should permeate all aspects of our Church life: it barely suffices to provide meager subsidies to a small number of newly established communities.

The missionary nature of the Church has wider implications. In spite of the sizable growth of Orthodox theological and spiritual literature in the English language, an Orthodox presence is still sadly lacking on university campuses. Having been recently present in Dallas, Texas, at the annual convention of the American Academy of Religion, which groups several hundred college religion teachers throughout the country, I became aware once more of the practically total absence of any Orthodox presence or challenge in their midst. "Eastern Christianity" is barely mentioned, and always in the context of the study of the early Christian centuries. Today, it appears only as a vestigial survival preserved in the local traditions of some ethnic groups.

So, before Orthodoxy is to become a real challenge on the contemporary religious scene, there is still a long way to go. Along this way lies our obligation not only to understand the true dimensions of our own faith, but also to assume that which is true and positive among others. Also along the way is the need for us to recognize that "mission" always starts with our neighbors—all of them. Having sometimes pierced the walls which have hidden Orthodoxy within Slavic or Mediterranean ghettoized enclaves, and reached to English-speaking whites, we have so far remained very far from Blacks and Hispanics (with very few exceptions).

All this lies along the way of true Orthodox mission. We have committed ourselves to it. Let us move ahead slowly, humbly, trusting in the power of God.

February, 1984

Women in the Church

The most extreme forms of the "women's lib" movement in our society may have subsided, but the issue of how to define and how to realize in practice the obvious affirmations of the Christian faith about the image of God in every human being, about the "royal priesthood" of the entire laity of the Church, and about the particular and distinct ministries of men and women, remains with us.

Modern Orthodox theology has done very little to answer the questions raised in this regard. And I begin to think that this relative silence—based on instinctive traditionalism and respect for the Church as she has existed for ages—is that which providentially saves us from doubtful improvisation or, worse, downright heresy. This does not mean that one should remain silent forever or consider that all the traditions (with a small "t") inherited from medieval Byzantium are necessarily to be identified with Holy Tradition itself. But theological reflection demands time: if improvised, it can easily take the shape either of gut-conservatism or irresponsible liberalism.

Where theological reflection—and eventual definition—is particularly needed is in the entire sphere of sacramental leadership—i.e., the priesthood—to which women have no access. I personally suspect that the definition will have to include not only the reference to Christ's manhood (which, in itself, may not be a sufficient argument), but the necessary association of Christian priesthood with the God-established and biblical model of "fatherhood"—not a "privilege" at all, but a great personal dimension of human life, which cannot be fulfilled by a mother. (But who can say that motherhood is "inferior" to fatherhood, morally, humanly, spiritually?)

As this theological task is being accomplished, there are other areas—the entire area which legitimately and unquestionably is the privilege of the entire people of God—where women, belonging to the Church, must, both proudly and humbly, fulfill their calling. They are irreplaceable in the family, but all the lay activities in the Church must be, and actually are, open to them as well: parochial, diocesan and national responsibilities in education, writing, intellectual and spiritual leadership.... Has our Church become so clericalized that one has to be a priest to be really useful? If this is the case, it is the entire structure and mentality of our Church which are at stake, not the single issue of women's ordination.

In any case, Holy Church, apostolic and catholic, deserves our confidence, our respect. Church issues will not be solved by slogans. It is a real blessing—and a sign of its truth and authenticity—that our Orthodoxy (in spite of its obvious historical weaknesses) has been able so far to avoid hasty revolutions. Let us work for the future, searching the *mind of the Church,* because she is the temple of the Spirit.

July, 1983

The Laity Includes Men and Women

The Church is composed of the entire people of God, men and women. The term "laity," which we use to designate the entire membership of the Church, comes from the Greek work *laos,* which means "people"—particularly the chosen people, who were selected by God himself to be His witnesses and His servants.

Therefore, there cannot be any difference in dignity and importance between men and women in the Church: both men and women enjoy all the duties, all the responsibilities and all the privileges which belong to the laity. There is no difference in the way they are baptized, chrismated and the way they enter the fellowship of the Body of Christ through communion. For historical reasons which would be difficult to describe here, the laity as a whole has been long excluded from active responsibility in Church life. In the Old World, until quite recently, lay people were simply "coming" to church for devotional purposes, but the clergy alone was responsible for all forms of welfare, administration or leadership. With the current—and fortunate—revival of conciliarity (of which the famous Moscow Council of 1917-1918 is the most characteristic witness), the Orthodox Church has returned to the original Christian practice of co-responsibility of both clergy and laity for the life of the Church. Clearly, the Orthodox faith could not envisage any progress in this country of America without making full use of the essential aspect of the Orthodox doctrine of the Church. And clearly, when one speaks of "lay" participation in Church life, one means the participation of both men and women.

The All-American Council in Detroit gave a final sanction to this indisputable principle. This does not mean, however, that the functions of men and women are always interchange-able in the various ministries within the Church, as they are not interchangeable in life in general. A woman, the holy Virgin Mary, became the Mother of God incarnate: no man is hailed as being "more honorable than the Cherubim." Furthermore, God has no earthly father.... This does not mean, however, that fatherhood, as such, does not exist anymore: indeed, it exists in the Church, as it exists in the family, and it cannot be realized by a woman, just as the virtue and grace of motherhood are not accessible to a man. The same can be said of such unique experiences of life, as being (or having) a brother, or being (or having) a sister, which are proper to one sex only, and which make life truly human, and beautiful, and happy, and enjoyable...

Let us preserve the precious gifts of unity and diversity, of equality and functionality, which were created by God in the beginning, which can be assumed into the eternal King-dom of God, if only we are seeking that Kingdom and struggle for it as the ultimate goal and meaning of our lives.

December, 1980